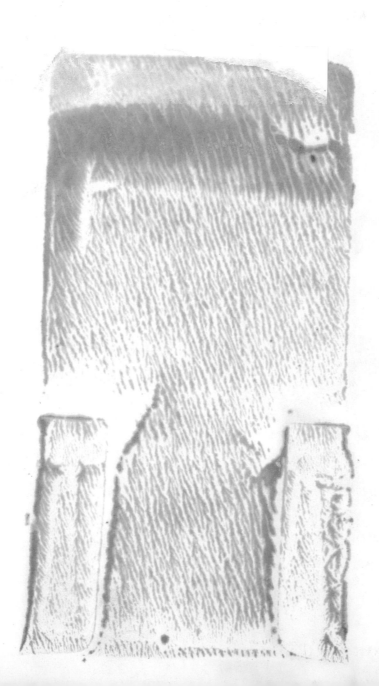

THE AMERICAN CHAIR

1630-1890

THE
AMERICAN CHAIR
1630-1890

BY

MARION DAY IVERSON

ILLUSTRATED BY
ERNEST DONNELLY

Hastings House Publishers   New York

TO C. JAY

I had three chairs in my house; one for solitude, two for friendship, three for society.

THOREAU

CONTENTS

PREFACE

CHAIRS have been called an index of furniture styles because anyone who has a knowledge of chair design can also identify many other furniture forms. On the pages that follow there is an account of the changing styles of chairs since the time of our first English colonists.

But chairs, like the other possessions of our founding fathers, are better understood in the light of personalities, writings and events contemporary to them. To become aware of this background, we look first at the man believed to have owned the chair originally and then at the chair itself. As we trace the styles in this way, through nearly three centuries, we are reminded of the traditions of our nation and of the cultural heritage of its people.

M.D.I.

ACKNOWLEDGMENTS

THE research for *The American Chair* has been done, for the most part, at libraries in the Twin Cities, principally the Minnesota Historical Society in St. Paul and the public library in Minneapolis. The books that are available on their shelves, especially those published long before Minnesota was even a Territory, have never ceased to astonish as well as to serve me. To the many librarians who have always been courteous, helpful and patient, I make a low bow. A personal word of gratitude must go to Miss Ruth Jedermann who, until her recent retirement, was head of the outstanding art department of the Minneapolis Public Library. For several years she befriended this venture while the plan for it gradually evolved.

That American museums and historic houses also are administered by persons of grace and good will became very evident during my quest for the photographs needed for Mr. Donnelly's drawings. Any number of directors and curators amiably answered the plea of an unknown Midwesterner, but they are not listed here because the photographs were obtained over a long period of time and some names might be omitted inadvertently. Their museums are named in the captions, as are the few private owners who provided me with photographs of chairs either now or formerly in their possession.

I want to express my particular obligation to Mr. Charles C. Wall, superintendent of Mount Vernon, and to Mrs. Helen Maggs Fede, the curator there, and also to Mr. Worth Bailey, formerly research assistant to Mr. Wall. The Reverend Mr. Arthur Pierce Middleton, at one time director of research at Colonial Williamsburg, also gave me knowledgeable assistance.

Because this book is primarily about chairs, and in the interest of brevity, no footnotes were included for the biographical and historical sections. To the learned historians of America whose writings I have studied in preparing this data go my respect and my appreciation.

The advertisements from early newspapers come mostly from *The Arts and Crafts in New York, 1726-1776*, edited by Rita Susswein Gottesman; from two volumes of *Arts and Crafts in Philadelphia, Maryland and South Carolina*, edited by the late Alfred Coxe Prime; and from *The Arts and Crafts in New England*, edited by the late George Francis Dow. I have benefited immeasurably from their time-consuming and painstaking efforts.

The Macmillan Company gave permission to have drawings made of a number of chairs from *Furniture Treasury* by Wallace Nutting. Miss Esther R. Svendson of Framingham, Massachusetts, thoughtfully supplied some of Mr. Nutting's original photographs now in her possession. Figure 38 was taken from *Colonial Furniture in America* by Luke Vincent Lockwood, with the permission of Book Sales, Incorporated. Besides the above comprehensive works on the subject of American furniture by Nutting and Lockwood, there is a third that is of great value to me as well as to other students and collectors. This is *American Antique Furniture: A Book for Amateurs,* brought out in 1937 by Edgar G. Miller, Jr.

The many references to *Antiques* Magazine in the footnotes give only a hint of the treasure stored in its issues. To Miss Alice Winchester, the editor, I am deeply beholden for her competent criticism of my manuscript, her gentle prodding toward its completion and the Foreword with which she has honored this printed volume. Mrs. Edith Gaines, copy editor of *Antiques,* has also proven herself a good friend.

Miss Narcisse Chamberlain of Hastings House has edited my copy with skill and precision. Moreover, she has been genial and gracious in our voluminous correspondence and personal association. For a decade and more Miss Hazel Anderson has patiently transcribed my scrawling pages of longhand to well-ordered pages of typewritten manuscript.

The drawings in Nutting's *Furniture Treasury III* have always held me in absorbed enchantment. They are artistic in feeling, yet honest in interpretation and the decorative details are easily observed. Imagine, then, my satisfaction when Mr. Donnelly, after reading a portion of the manuscript, agreed to illustrate *The American Chair.* He is a gentleman of Irish birth and boyhood, but he has acquired an unusual appreciation of American craftsmanship; somehow he carries his love of fine furniture to the drawing board. To say more about his gifts is quite unnecessary—they are so apparent to anyone who so much as glances between the covers of this book.

MARION DAY IVERSON
AUGUST 23, 1957

FOREWORD

ANTIQUES are history. That is a fundamental belief of most students and lovers of antiques but one not often clearly elucidated. For while it is easy to say in general terms—as I am fond of doing myself—that antiques are a tangible record of the past and reveal an intimate aspect of the way our people lived, it is more difficult to show just how a specific antique object, say an eighteenth-century chair, is a part of eighteenth-century history.

That is what Mrs. Iverson does in this book. She tells the story of the chair in terms of specific chairs owned and sat in by actual people whose names have come down in the annals of our history. What she tells about those people and the scenes and events they knew are an answer to the old wish, "If only that chair could talk!"

This book is, however, far more than a George-Washington-slept-here sort of thing. The seats of the mighty that Mrs. Iverson considers represent all the major types of chair made in America from the days of the earliest colonies to the time of the Civil War. The chair itself may be taken as the exemplar of furniture design: it is a universal form which shows in its construction, proportion, and decoration all the changing styles in their endless sequence. Thus, by tracing its evolution in America, which she does concisely, palatably, and reliably, Mrs. Iverson has also sketched in the broader pattern of development in other forms of furniture and even in others of the decorative arts. Her information on textiles used in upholstery, for example, is ample and valuable. Her text is illuminated by countless quotations from contemporary documents which not only substantiate her statements but give color and immediacy to the whole story of the chair.

The drawings by Ernest Donnelly are admirably suited to illustrate this text. Their sensitive line and accurate detail bring out, even more clearly than photographs could do, not only the stylistic sequence of chair design but also the many fine points that Mrs. Iverson has worked into her presentation.

Specialists in any field are apt to develop their own approach, a concern with minute problems, even a sort of cryptic language. Antiquarians, convinced though they are of the historical importance of antiques, are all too prone to concentrate on fine points of craftsmanship, and to neglect to link these up with their broader social background. In this story of the chair in America, Mrs. Iverson has achieved a happy combination of the scholarly and the human, and made a welcome contribution to our cultural history.

ALICE WINCHESTER
Editor, ANTIQUES Magazine

CHAPTER ONE

Chairs of the Seventeenth Century

WAINSCOT
TURNED
CROMWELLIAN
CANE

Fig. 1 WAINSCOT ARMCHAIR
presumed to have belonged to
John Winthrop, Jr. (1606-1676)
(Wesleyan University, Middletown, Connecticut)

1. *WAINSCOT* (*c.* 1630-*c.* 1680)

Oak

> *In the hall: one longe Table, one stoole, two formes . . . three chaiers*
> *& six cushins . . . In the parlor: one table with six joyned stooles . . .*
> *3 chaiers & 8 cushins.*
>
> Inventory of Richard Lumpkyn
Ipswich, Massachusetts, 1642

A PROMISING young man was aboard the ship *Lyon* when it sailed into Boston Harbor in November, 1631. He was John Winthrop, Jr., son and namesake of the governor of Massachusetts Bay Colony. He had attended Trinity College, Dublin, and had been admitted to the bar in London. Service in the Royal Navy followed and after that more than a year of travel on the Continent.

For all his legal training the younger Winthrop's chief interest was science and he is thought to have had the largest scientific library in seventeenth-century America. Shortly after his arrival he undertook a number of enterprises such as producing salt from sea water, mining lead and developing ironworks.* Colonists soon learned of his knowledge of medicine and came to him from near and far for remedies for their ailments.

He founded Ipswich, Massachusetts, in 1633 and later other "plantations" in both Massachusetts and Connecticut. Winthrop was a genial, able leader and was often offered inducements to live in different localities. Once, New Haven settlers tried to attract him by presenting to him and his family a house, furniture, supplies of candles, wheat and firewood, as well as "a cleanly, thrifty maide-servant." Even Peter Stuyvesant urged him to start a settlement on Long Island near Manhattan.

* When * appears, see Appendix for a list of historic houses and museums mentioned in the text that are open to the public; places where many of the chairs in this book are to be seen are also listed.

In 1657 John Winthrop, Jr. was elected governor of Connecticut and three years later he went to England with a message of loyalty to Charles II, recently restored to the throne. He was a skillful, polished diplomat and the King granted Connecticut a liberal charter. It was so liberal that a quarter of a century later colonists hid it in the Charter Oak at Hartford in order to keep it.

The younger Winthrop, by tradition, occupied this wainscot chair (Fig. 1) when he was inaugurated governor of Connecticut. As in other wainscot chairs, its massive size and seat high above the floor give an impressive and thronelike appearance. Wainscot originally was the finest oak imported in England from Holland and Germany. Walls were lined with it and wall lining, usually paneled, came to be known as wainscoting. Chairs, chests, cupboards and other furniture made of this same paneled oak are called wainscot.

In the early seventeenth century there was not yet the specialized skill of cabinetmaking and the same "joiner" who did the wainscoting and other woodwork also made furniture. He used mortise and tenon and other joints. In early records a wainscot chair is often called a joined chair.

Only a score or so of the early wainscot chairs are still in existence in this country. Some are plain (Fig. 2), others carved. The two most handsomely carved (Fig. 3) once belonged to Thomas Dennis, a joiner who first bought property in Ipswich in 1663.[1] The John Winthrop, Jr. inaugural chair has carving and other characteristics of the work of Nicholas Disbrowe (1612-1683), a joiner of Hartford, Connecticut.

Joiners were numbered among our earliest colonists, but like other craftsmen they had to spend much time, at first, tilling the soil. However, John Winthrop, Jr.'s sister, Mrs. Samuel Dudley of Ipswich, confidently sent to Boston for a child's chair in 1636. She expected it to be made "a fortnight hence," when she had arranged for "Goodman Button's Boat" to bring it to Ipswich.[2]

The colonists of Massachusetts Bay apparently were not idle, because in 1642 one of them was writing that they lived in "orderly, fair and well-built houses, well furnished many of them."[3] A well-furnished house at that time did not necessarily mean that it had several chairs, since they were not yet in common use even in England. Many colonists sat on joined stools (Fig. 4), or benches, also called short and long forms. They had "cushion" stools too, presumably those with upholstered seats. When there was only one chair in a household, it was for the head of the family or his guest—definitely a seat of honor. At meetings the chair was used by the person in authority and that is why a presiding officer, even today, is asked to "take the chair."

4

Fig. 2
WAINSCOT chair with no carving, said to have belonged to **Governor Leete** of Connecticut (Stone House, Guilford, Connecticut—from Nutting's *Furniture Treasury*). The John Winthrop, Jr. chair (Fig. 1) may once have had a crest like this one over the paneled back.

[1] Irving P. Lyon, "The Oak Furniture of Ipswich, Massachusetts," *Antiques,* November, 1937.
[2] *Winthrop Papers,* III, 242.
[3] *Johnson's Wonder-Working Providence,* ed. Jameson, pp. 211-12.

Fig. 3
CARVED WAINSCOT chair (now the President's Chair,
Bowdoin College, Brunswick, Maine) once owned by
Thomas Dennis, a joiner known to have carved
other furniture. A similar Dennis chair is now at the
Essex Institute, Salem, Massachusetts.

6

Fig. 4
JOINED STOOL, or short form, sometimes called a joint
stool, used when there were few chairs (Greenwood
Gift, Smithsonian Institution, Washington, D.C.).
The colonists also had benches, or long forms.

7

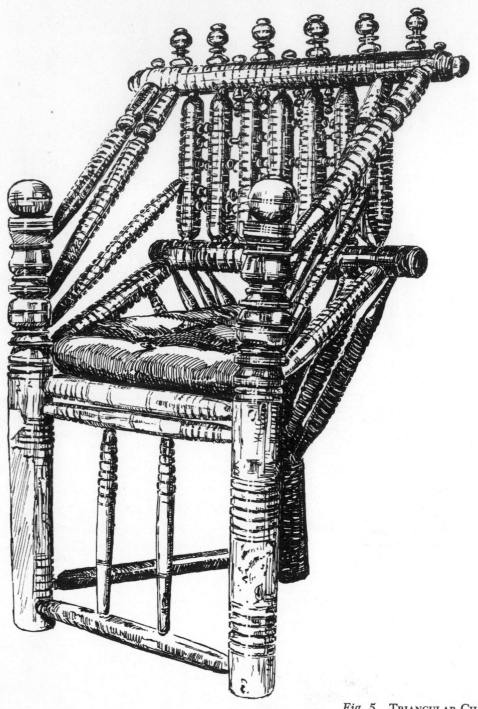

Fig. 5 TRIANGULAR CHAIR
believed to be of English origin.
(The President's Chair, Harvard University,
Cambridge, Massachusetts)

2. *TURNED CHAIRS*

TRIANGULAR (*c.* 1630-*c.* 1660)
Oak, Ash, other woods

SLAT-BACK (*c.* 1630 to the present day)
Maple and other woods

> *Funny old chair with seat like wedge,*
> *Sharp behind and broad front edge,—*
> *One of the oddest of human things,*
> *Turned all over with knobs and rings,—*
> *But heavy, and wide, and deep, and grand,—*
> *Fit for the worthies of the land,—*
> Oliver Wendell Holmes

A FAIRLY accurate picture of the interiors of the first American houses is disclosed in the inventories of the colonists' belongings made when their estates were settled.[1] Listed are such widely separated items as ruffs and halberds, "sizzers" and "winescott" chests.

In inventories "chair" is spelled in many ways—chayer, chaier, chaire, cheere and cheyre—and different spellings of the word often are found in the same inventory. "Great" and "elbow" chairs were armchairs, and "small" chairs were side chairs. Appraisers were not always as explicit as they might have been and entries like "1 Cheire" or "2 great wooden Chaires" are not very revealing as to their style.

There are, of course, a good many other documents which yield information about the household goods of the American colonial family. Deeds, wills and court litigations sometimes tell us much. There was, for example, the action instituted by the children of Mrs. Henry Dunster, wife of the first president of Harvard College. Depositions by two of her nine former servants give vivid descriptions of the elaborate furnishings she possessed.

Letters, too, are of value, sometimes even those from another country. In England Horace Walpole, who was a great collector, wrote a friend about the

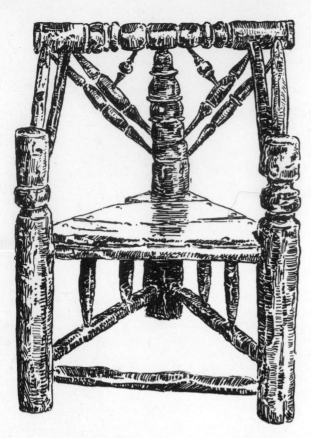

Fig. 6

TRIANGULAR or "buffet" chair from Topsfield, Massachusetts (Greenwood Gift,
Smithsonian Institution, Washington,
D.C.). This turned chair with wooden
seat is of undetermined 16th- or early
17th-century origin and was probably
brought to America by the first settlers.

"ancient" chairs he was seeking in 1761. Someone he knew had "picked up a
whole cloister full of old chairs in Hertfordshire . . . one by one, here and there
in farm-houses." They were "of wood, the seats triangular, the backs, arms and
legs loaded with turnery."[2]

A triangular chair "loaded with turnery" at Harvard University is believed
to be of English origin (Fig. 5). For about two centuries the president of the
college has sat in this chair while conferring degrees at commencement ceremonies. There is no evidence that it was a bequest of the Reverend Ebenezer
Turell of the class of 1721, as suggested by Dr. Oliver Wendell Holmes in "Par-
son Turell's Legacy." However, Edward Holyoke, president from 1737 to 1769,
had his portrait painted while seated in the chair.

The buffet chairs found in a few of the early inventories are believed to
have been triangular. Buffet comes from the early English word "bofet," meaning a three-footed stool, and has no connection with the French word meaning
cupboard or sideboard.[3] John Baldwin of Salem, Massachusetts, apparently
liked them. He had "thre bufett chaiers" in 1673.[4] The triangular chairs in this
country today probably could be counted on the fingers of one hand. The ancient

Fig. 7
SLAT-BACK chair with square posts, earlier than slat-back chairs with turned posts (*Antiques,* October, 1931). Similar chairs were depicted in European paintings of the 15th century.

one at the Smithsonian Institution came from Topsfield, Massachusetts (Fig. 6).

In European paintings dating back to the fifteenth century we discover both triangular and slat-back chairs. The first slat-back chairs had square rather than round posts (Fig. 7). The posts of a chair are the four uprights that form the back and legs. Only about six crude, square-post, slat-back chairs are now known to have survived in America.[5] Their rounded stretchers were shaped by a drawshave.

All other slat-back chairs are turned. Like triangular chairs, they are made almost entirely of "turnery" or turned wood, wood that has been shaped by a cutting tool while being rotated on a lathe. Such chairs usually were made by a turner rather than by a joiner. On square-post, slat-back chairs the slats were flat; on turned slat-backs they were bent outward for greater comfort. The shape of the slat had several variations. Slats with quarter circles cut from the ends of the upper edge are frequently seen on seventeenth-century chairs (Fig. 8).

Colonists apparently liked furniture with more than one use. A table became a chair when the hinged top was turned up to form the back (Fig. 9). Will Wright of Plymouth had "a little chaire table" in 1633[6] and Nathaniel Warren, another Pilgrim, had three of them in 1667.[7] The settle, a wooden settee, some-

11

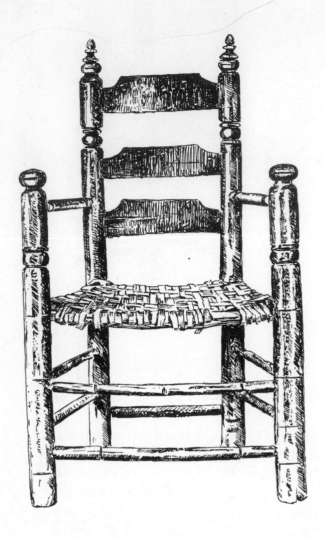

Fig. 8
SLAT-BACK chair with turned posts and splint seat (Wadsworth Atheneum, Hartford, Connecticut—from Nutting's *Furniture Treasury*). The heavy posts, the turnings and the shape of the slats are marks of an early chair.

times was a settle bed; then the seat could be unhooked and fall forward to form a bed (Figs. 18, 19). A settle and two settle beds were owned by Elder William Brewster of Plymouth before 1644.[8]

[1] In selecting chairs for illustration, their artistic merit has been the primary consideration, their historic interest secondary (with the exception of Thomas Jefferson's windsor, Number 11). It has been impossible, in six instances, to find acceptable chairs to represent certain furniture styles that also have historic association. Therefore, here, as in Numbers 7, 8, 9, 13 and 14, a related subject has replaced the usual biographical sketch. M.D.I.

[2] *Letters of Horace Walpole,* ed. Cunningham, III, 429.

[3] Luke V. Lockwood, *Colonial Furniture in America,* II, 7; and *The Oxford English Dictionary.*

[4] *Essex County Probate Records* (Massachusetts), ed. Dow, II, 383.

[5] Irving P. Lyon, "Square-Post Slat-Back Chairs," *Antiques,* October, 1931.

[6] *Mayflower Descendant,* I, 205.

[7] *Ibid.,* II, 39.

[8] *Ibid.,* III, 15-27.

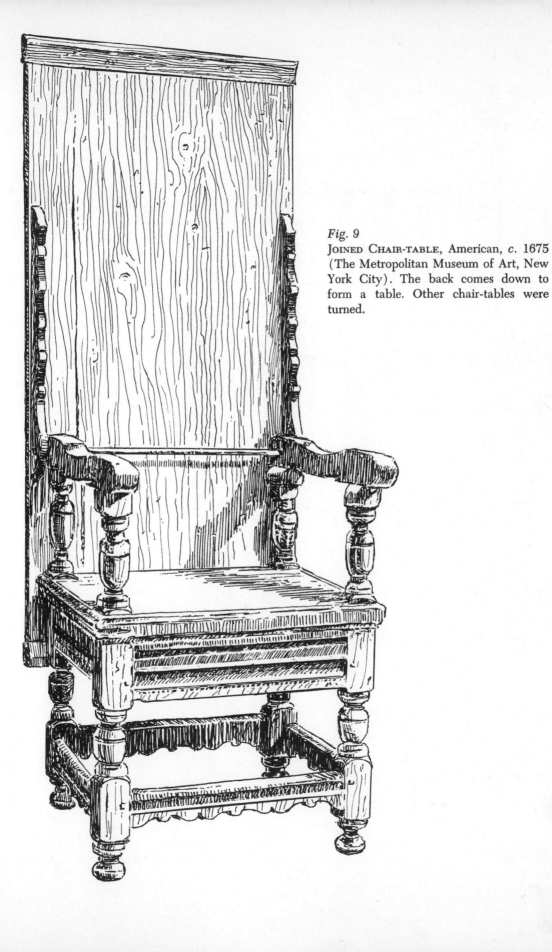

Fig. 9
JOINED CHAIR-TABLE, American, *c.* 1675
(The Metropolitan Museum of Art, New
York City). The back comes down to
form a table. Other chair-tables were
turned.

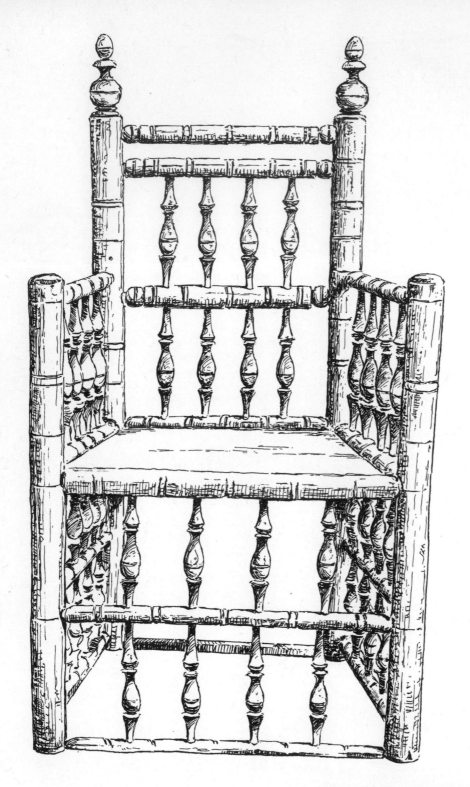

Fig. 10 BREWSTER ARMCHAIR
presumed to have belonged to
William Bradford (1590-1657)
(Pilgrim Society, Pilgrim Hall, Plymouth, Massachusetts)

3. TURNED CHAIRS

CARVER (*c.* 1620-*c.* 1700)
Ash, Maple, other woods

BREWSTER (*c.* 1620-*c.* 1700)
Ash, Maple, other woods

> *Four Joint stooles . . . one cushin stool . . . two flag chaires . . . one 3 Square chaire [triangular?] . . . fower Lether chaires . . . one lether Chaire . . . a flag bottome chaire . . . cushion stool . . . five Chayres.*
> Inventory of Richard Jacobs
> Ipswich, Massachusetts, 1672

JOHN CARVER, "a well approved gentleman," was chosen governor of the Colony after the Pilgrims signed the Mayflower Compact on November 11, 1620. Of the hundred or so passengers, only about fifty survived the first winter. Nevertheless, when Chief Massasoit and sixty warriors suddenly appeared in March, 1621, to make their first visit, the ailing Pilgrims made a brave attempt to receive them with fitting ceremony.

Captain Standish met the chief "at the brook with half a dozen muskateers" and conducted him to a partially completed house. "Instantly" Governor Carver appeared "with drum and trumpet after him." Massasoit "marveled much" at their trumpet and intimated that he would like to buy a sword and armor. Before Massasoit left, he and Governor Carver signed a treaty of peace.

The Governor lived less than a month and William Bradford, just thirty-one, was selected to take his place. By autumn the Pilgrims were "all well recovered in health & strength, and had all things in good plenty." Governor Bradford set apart several days for Thanksgiving "so we might, after a special manner, rejoice together after we had gathered the fruit of our labors."

He sent four men hunting and in one day they returned with "as much fowl as, with a little help beside, served the company almost a week." The company

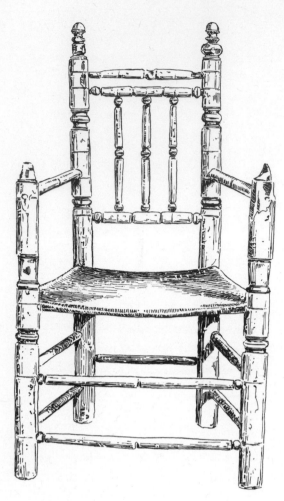

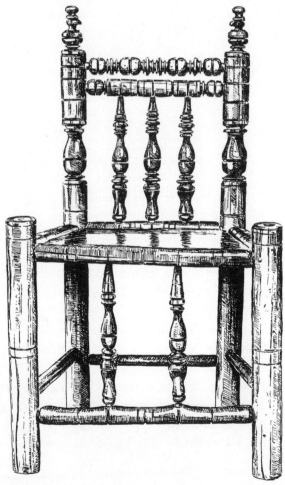

Fig. 11
CARVER chair said to have belonged to **Governor Carver** (Pilgrim Society, Pilgrim Hall, Plymouth, Massachusetts). It has three horizontal rails and three vertical spindles in the back and elaborately turned finials on the back posts.

Fig. 12
BREWSTER child's chair (Henry N. Flynt, Heritage Foundation, Deerfield, Massachusetts). Brewster chairs usually have more spindles in the back than Carver chairs and spindles under the arms or seat, or both (Fig. 10). This is an important early child's chair made of American oak.

included Massasoit who came this time with ninety men. They presented the Pilgrims with several deer.

Elder Brewster, thirty years Bradford's senior, no doubt delighted in the holiday. He was "of a very cherful spirite, very sociable and pleasante amongst his friends." The Elder also was a man of learning and his library numbered some three hundred volumes.

Two chairs exhibited at Pilgrim Hall, Plymouth, are believed to have been owned by Governor Carver and Elder Brewster. All chairs made like them are spoken of as Carver or Brewster chairs. Backs of Carver chairs are made up of three horizontal rails and three vertical spindles; both rails and spindles are turned (Fig. 11). Brewster chairs have a greater number of spindles in the back and, in addition, have spindles under the arm or under the seat, or in both places (Fig. 10).

Carver and Brewster chairs have the heavy turned posts and the elaborate finials of the early seventeenth-century slat-back chairs. The finials are the decorative turnings at the top of the back posts. Ball or mushroom turning frequently crowned the front posts (Fig. 8), but on the chairs of Governor Carver and Elder Brewster they have been partially worn off or whittled away.

Descendants of Governor Bradford have recently given his chair of the Brewster type to the Pilgrim Society. In three centuries it has had so much wear that the bottom stretcher is on the floor. No remnants of ball or mushroom turning remain on the front posts. When the Governor's estate was settled in 1657, he owned eleven chairs besides forms, stools and a settle. This chair supposedly was one of his six "great" chairs. His two "great Carved Chaires" and his "small carved Chaire" we presume were wainscot.[1]

Seats of turned chairs usually were of rush or splint, although a few had seats of wood (Figs. 10, 12). Splint seats were woven from the inner bark of certain trees, often the basswood, also called the linden (Fig. 8). They are listed in inventories as bass or bass-bottomed chairs.

Rush seats were used more commonly than splint ones. Rushes, known as reeds or flags, were gathered from marshes and cured before being woven into seats (Fig. 23). They were listed as rush, flag or straw-bottomed chairs. John Atwood of Plymouth owned "2 flagg bottome chaires" in 1643,[2] and Captain George Corwin of Salem, Massachusetts, had five "Stra bottomed Chaires" and one "old Wicker Chaire" in 1684.[3]

No early wicker chair is known to exist, but they were in the inventories of

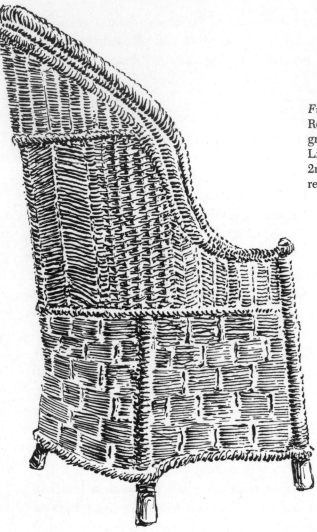

Fig. 13

ROMAN WICKER chair (from a photograph, courtesy of the Minneapolis Public Library). This chair dates from about the 2nd century A.D. and is carved on a tomb relief at Neumagen, near Trèves, France.

many colonists.[4] Centuries before a wicker chair had been carved on a tomb relief in France (Fig. 13). Flemish artists of the seventeenth century depicted wicker chairs (Fig. 14), possibly similar to those in America.

[1] *Mayflower Descendant,* II, 228-34.
[2] *Ibid.,* V, 153-9.
[3] George Francis Dow, *Every Day Life in the Massachusetts Bay Colony,* p. 279.
[4] Marion Day Iverson, "Wickerwork in the Seventeenth Century," *Antiques,* March, 1954.

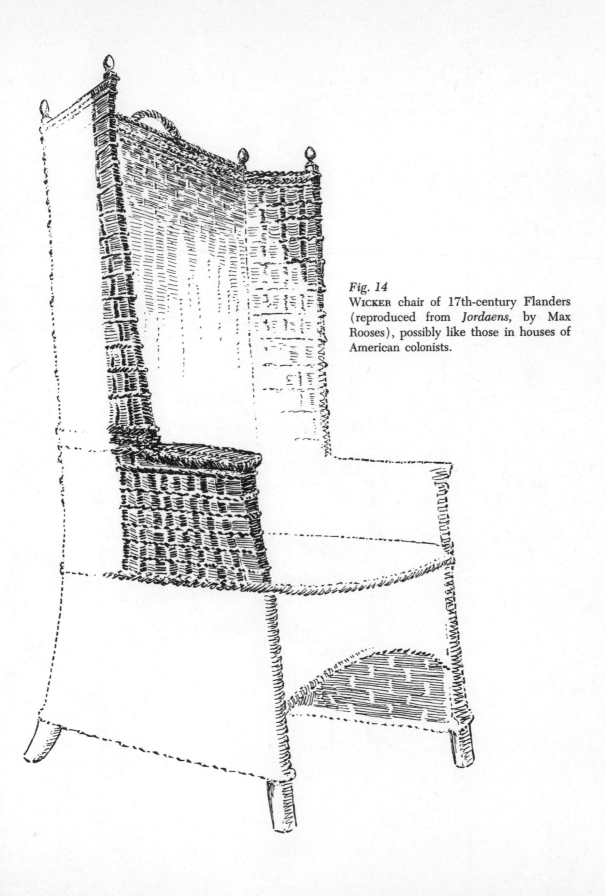

Fig. 14
WICKER chair of 17th-century Flanders (reproduced from *Jordaens,* by Max Rooses), possibly like those in houses of American colonists.

Fig. 15 CROMWELLIAN CHAIR
presumed to have belonged to
Roger Williams (*c.* 1603-1683)
(From a photograph, courtesy of John H. Schmuck,
Naugatuck, Connecticut, descendant of Roger Williams)

4. *CROMWELLIAN* (*c.* 1640-*c.* 1700)

Maple and other woods

> *12 Turkey work chaires . . . 6 lether chaires . . . 4 straw bottom chaires . . . 1 old low lether chaire . . . 6 old joyne stooles . . . 6 searge chaires, 3 chaires & 1 cushon.*
>
> Inventory of Hilliard Veren, Jr.
> Salem, Massachusetts, 1680

ROGER WILLIAMS, a scholarly graduate of Cambridge, was hailed as "a godly minister" when he arrived in Massachusetts Bay in 1631. Soon he was being called "contentious." He refused the pastorate in Boston because the Puritans there had not completely separated from the Church of England and he differed with the colonists on other matters, including the interpretation of the Bible. Moreover, Williams questioned the right of the King to grant them land that had belonged to the Indians. By 1635 he was banished for having "dyvulged dyvers newe and dangerous opinions." His arrest was ordered, but Governor Winthrop sent him a secret warning and he fled to the wilderness. Later he recalled that he spent "fourteen weeks, in bitter winter season, not knowing what bread or bed did mean."

The following summer Roger Williams purchased land from the Indians to found Providence, Rhode Island. There he established freedom of worship, the initial step toward religious liberty in our nation. He proved to be of great assistance to those who had banished him, because he arbitrated successfully with the warring red men. He once referred to the Indians as "wild barbarous wretches," yet he befriended them. When he was in England in 1643, he published the first dictionary of their tongue.

This book and later ones on other subjects brought a distinction to Williams' name which has continued through the centuries. He seems to have had a flair for languages and while in London in 1652 practiced "the Hebrew, the Greeke, Latine, French and Dutch" with John Milton and other friends. In the interests of his colony he also had an intimate talk with Oliver Cromwell.

Roger Williams is said to have owned this upholstered chair without arms (Fig. 15). It has ball-and-block turned posts and a ball-and-ring turned front stretcher. This style has been called Cromwellian even though it was in vogue some years before and after the time of Cromwell and the Commonwealth. In Massachusetts, William Clarke of Salem[1] and Captain Thomas Coytemore of Boston[2] had similar chairs, upholstered in leather, prior to 1647.

The old records describe these chairs by their upholstery. In addition to leather chairs, there were serge, velvet, plush, silk, penniston and paragon chairs, and even sealskin chairs. Penniston and paragon were fabrics that are no longer made. Sometimes they are listed simply as cloth chairs. Many were wrought (needlework) or turkey-wrought or turkeywork chairs. Turkeywork resembled Turkish carpets and was made by drawing yarn through coarse material. It was then knotted and cut somewhat the way hooked rugs are fashioned.

In 1679 Benjamin Gibbs, a Boston mariner, had sixty-seven chairs and all but nine appear to have been Cromwellian. "Two dozen of turkey worke chaires" were in his hall, the principal room of a seventeenth-century dwelling. Seventeen leather and a like number of cloth chairs were in other rooms.[3] Comparatively few Cromwellian chairs are in existence today and it is believed that they were discarded when their upholstery became worn. Significant of wear and tear, perhaps, is the inventory of Mary Winslow of Plymouth who had "3 Chaires without Leathers" along with eleven leather chairs in 1679.[4] Chair frames were frequently listed in inventories.

Captain Kidd, the pirate, owned "two dozen single nailed leather cheares very old" in 1692, according to New York records.[5] The large-headed nails that decorated and secured the upholstery could be in "single" rows (Fig. 16) or double. Fringe sometimes trimmed chairs upholstered in fabric (Fig. 17), such as the "2 red cloath chaires with fringe" that belonged to William Paine of Boston in 1660.[6]

Upholstered chairs with higher backs than the Cromwellian were being made at this time but they are seldom found today. Because they were upholstered in the same materials as the Cromwellian, it is not often possible to distinguish in the records which is meant. But the appraisers of the worldly

Fig. 16
CROMWELLIAN chair, upholstered in leather secured by large-headed nails in a single row (Nutting's *Furniture Treasury*). Usually there were no finials; backs were low and seats often high from the floor.

goods of Captain William Tyng of Boston did make the distinction. Among the upholstered chairs in his hall in 1653 were "6 high back chaires and 2 lowe backe chaires."[7]

[1] *Essex County Probate,* I, 66.
[2] *Massachusetts Colonial Records,* ed. Shurtleff, II, 232.
[3] *Suffolk Deeds,* (Massachusetts), XI, 192-3.
[4] *Mayflower Descendant,* I, 70-1.
[5] Lockwood, *Colonial Furniture,* II, 27.
[6] Dow, *Every Day Life,* p. 261.
[7] Suffolk County Probate Records (Massachusetts), II, 138.

Fig. 17
CROMWELLIAN chair with fabric upholstery
trimmed with fringe (Wadsworth Atheneum, Hartford, Connecticut—from Nutting's
Furniture Treasury). There are no turnings
on the back posts or on the front stretcher as
in Fig. 16.

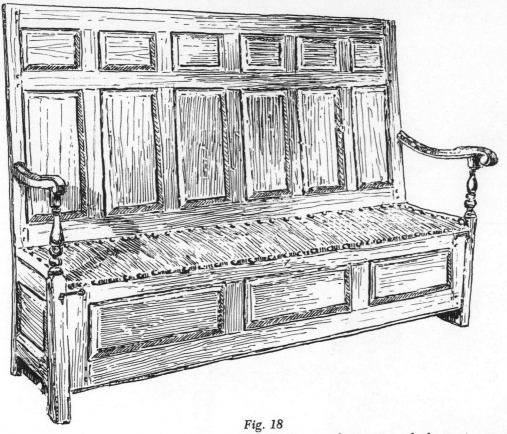

Fig. 18
SETTLE or wooden settee of the wainscot type
(Nutting's *Furniture Treasury*). This is a settle bed
like those owned by Elder Brewster and many other
early settlers.

Fig. 19
The settle bed, open.

Fig. 20 CANE ARMCHAIR
presumed to have belonged to
William Penn (1644-1718)
(*Antiques* Magazine, April, 1927)

5. *CANE CHAIRS* (*c.* 1675-*c.* 1725)

Walnut, Beech, Maple
Sometimes painted black

That there be provided to be set in the Councill Chamber [of the Capitol at Williamsburg] one Oval table . . . with two doz: arm'd Cain Chairs, one larger ditto, twenty-five green Cushions for the said Chairs stuft with hair, and a large Turkey work Carpet for the table.
Journals of the House of Burgesses of Virginia
April 9, 1703

WILLIAM PENN was expelled from Christ College, Oxford, in 1662 because of his views on religion. This greatly annoyed his father, Admiral Sir William Penn of the Royal Navy, who promptly sent him on a tour of the Continent. French court life and other influences seem to have had the desired effect, because two years later Samuel Pepys was recording in his diary that Sir William's son had returned a "most modish person, grown . . . a fine gentleman." But in 1667 Pepys noted that young Penn was "a Quaker again or some very melancholy thing."

It was in 1681 that Charles II granted him land in America in payment of a debt owed the late Admiral Penn. The Quaker planned carefully for his colonists in Delaware, New Jersey and Pennsylvania and he made two voyages to America, though he stayed in all less than four years.

While he was here Penn spent part of his time at Pennsbury Manor,* his country estate on the Delaware River some twenty-five miles above Philadelphia. After going back to England he sent letter after letter of instructions to his steward at Pennsbury. He expected to "bring much furniture" when he returned to this country in 1699, but he asked the steward to "get some wooden chairs of walnut with long backs."[1] He sent a joiner, a wheelwright, a gardener and carpenters to America to be employed at Pennsbury.

Fig. 21
The FLEMISH SCROLL carved on cane chairs took many forms and often was seen with the fleur-de-lis.

Penn was aboard ship in 1701, bound for Britain, when he wrote his secretary to "send all the household goods" from his town house in Philadelphia "up to Pennsbury."[2] Decades later, after many souvenirs had been taken from the unoccupied manor, the remaining furniture was sold or given away.

It is not surprising that today several cane chairs are alleged to have belonged to William Penn (Fig. 20). In his "best parlour" at Pennsbury he had "two tables, one couch, two great cane chairs and four small ditto, seven cushions—four of them satin, three others green plush, and sundries more." In the best chamber were "sundry" cane chairs, and twelve additional cane chairs were elsewhere in the manor.[3]

These elaborately carved chairs with cane in the backs and seats are believed to have been introduced to England by Charles II when he was restored to the throne in 1660. That is why they are sometimes called Charles II or Carolean chairs. They had been in vogue in the Continental countries where he had spent his exile.

Most often the design in the carving is the Flemish scroll (Fig. 21). It is carved around the panel of cane in the back and on the front stretcher. The Flemish scroll also forms the front legs (Fig. 22), and when the legs angle outward they are considered more desirable (Fig. 20). The shaped arm that curves downward and outward like those on the Penn chair is called a ramshorn arm.

28

Cane chairs evidently were in use in America a while before the 1680's, when they appeared in inventories of estates in Virginia,[4] Pennsylvania[4, 5] and Massachusetts.[6] They were still being made in one Philadelphia shop "after the best and newest fashion" as late as 1734.[7]

It is possible to know just when certain pieces of furniture were made from the cabinetmakers' labels, bills or other records, but the time that furniture styles became fashionable is rather vague. That is why *circa*, or its abbreviations *ca.* or *c.*, is placed before dates. When a new style appeared cabinetmakers did not at once stop making the old ones, and neither did their fellow craftsmen in England. The change was gradual and there was always a period when two styles overlapped.

Colonists who lived in or near cities with good harbors kept more closely in touch with the mother country than those in remote areas. Ships arrived with remarkable frequency and, at most, only a few months elapsed before the styles in London were known in America. Whether or not they were immediately taken up depended upon the taste and wealth of the colonist and his desire to keep up-to-date.

[1] John F. Watson, *Annals of Philadelphia and Pennsylvania*, II, 104.
[2] Samuel Janney, *Life of William Penn*, p. 439.
[3] Watson, *Annals*, II, 104-6.
[4] Lockwood, *Colonial Furniture*, II, 32.
[5] Irving W. Lyon, *The Colonial Furniture of New England*, p. 155.
[6] *Ibid.*, p. 153.
[7] Alfred Coxe Prime, *Arts and Crafts in Philadelphia, Maryland and South Carolina*, I, 167-8.

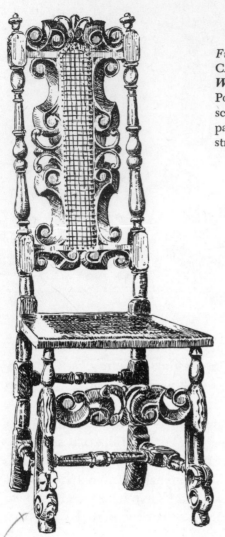

Fig. 22
CANE chair said to have been owned by *Sir William Pepperrell* (Moffat-Ladd House, Portsmouth, New Hampshire). The Flemish scroll and fleur-de-lis are carved around the panel of cane in the back and on the front stretcher. Flemish scrolls form the front legs.

Fig. 23
CANE chair with spiral turnings and a rush seat which perhaps replaced worn cane (Washington's Headquarters, Morristown National Historical Park, Morristown, New Jersey). Cane chairs with backs of average height like this one are believed to have preceded those with extremely high backs.

6. CANE CHAIRS (*c.* 1675-*c.* 1725)

Walnut, Beech, Maple

Sometimes painted black

> At Vendue *[auction], by Mr Daniel Goffe, at the* Sun Tavern *in Dock Square, . . . Cane Chairs, Couches, Sconces, Tea-Tables, Pewter, New and Second Handed, one Clock, Ruggs, Quilts, some Pictures, together with Sundry other things.*
>
> New England Journal
> (Boston) March 20, 1727

WILLIAM PEPPERRELL of Kittery Point, Maine, was one of the five or more colonists knighted by English kings. Curiously, three were named William. Besides Pepperrell, there was William Phipps of Maine and William Johnson of New York. Others were John Randolph and Peyton Skipworth of Virginia.

As William Pepperrell grew up at Kittery Point he became associated in business with his father, for whom he was named. They built ships and carried on extensive trade with Europe, the West Indies and our southern colonies. They greatly increased their fortune by investing profits in Maine land that grew rapidly in value. Maine was then a part of Massachusetts and, in time, young Pepperrell was chosen a member of the Royal Governor's Council. Eventually he became its president, an office he held for eighteen years.

Pepperrell had been colonel of the Maine regiment and when the New England forces made their expedition against the French in Nova Scotia, in 1745, he was given supreme command. Their capture of Louisburg, on Cape Breton Island, was the first British victory of any consequence in America. Pepperrell returned a hero and was soon knighted by King George II. While visiting England in 1749, he was received by the King and honored by the city of London.

In America Sir William and Lady Pepperrell sought to maintain a style of living befitting his title. He often dressed in scarlet trimmed with gold lace. Their house was lavishly furnished, their equipage expensive, and they, like William Penn at Pennsbury, possessed an elaborate barge manned by a uniformed crew.

Two cane chairs said to have belonged to Sir William Pepperrell long have been on exhibition at Portsmouth, New Hampshire,* just across the Piscataqua River from Kittery Point, Maine (Fig. 22). Another cane chair is spoken of as Lady Pepperrell's (Fig. 24).* Until recently it was upholstered on the back and seat, as were so many others after the original cane gave way. But occasionally no evidence of cane can be found underneath the upholstery because a few chairs in this style were upholstered to begin with, as a rule in leather (Fig. 54).

The three different types of cane chair can be identified by looking at the crest or ornamental top rail across the top of the back (Fig. 25). The first type has the crest between the posts as on the William Penn and William Pepperrell chairs. This is the earliest type and the one with the most carving. The chairs with backs of average height (Fig. 23) are believed to have preceded those with high backs—the highest ever made.

The second type has the crest above the posts like Lady Pepperrell's chair. The crest is the only carving on the back, but sometimes the front legs and front stretcher are carved (Fig. 26). At other times the legs are turned as on the third type. On the turned leg, the so-called Spanish foot makes its first appearance (Fig. 27).

A crest without carving is seen on the cane chair of the third type. It is shaped of molded wood of the same width as the molded wood that forms the stiles (Fig. 28). The stile is the part of the back post above the seat. When it is turned, it is called a post, when not turned, a stile.

Just how often the early colonists sent to Britain for their furniture is not easily determined. In the records of Samuel Sewall, grandfather of Lady Pepperrell, there is a suggestion that most Massachusetts furniture was made in the colony. He became a Boston merchant in 1675 and fifty-three articles in his bills of invoice during his first years in business have been tabulated by the quantity ordered of each. Chairs, the only furniture noted, were fifty-second, next to the last on the list.[1] The furniture exported to the colonies was recorded in Great Britain after 1697.[2]

In 1719 Sewall, by then chief justice of Massachusetts, sent to England for furnishings for his daughter, Judith, a prospective bride. Included were "A Duzen of good black Walnut Chairs, fine Cane, with a Couch, A Duzen of

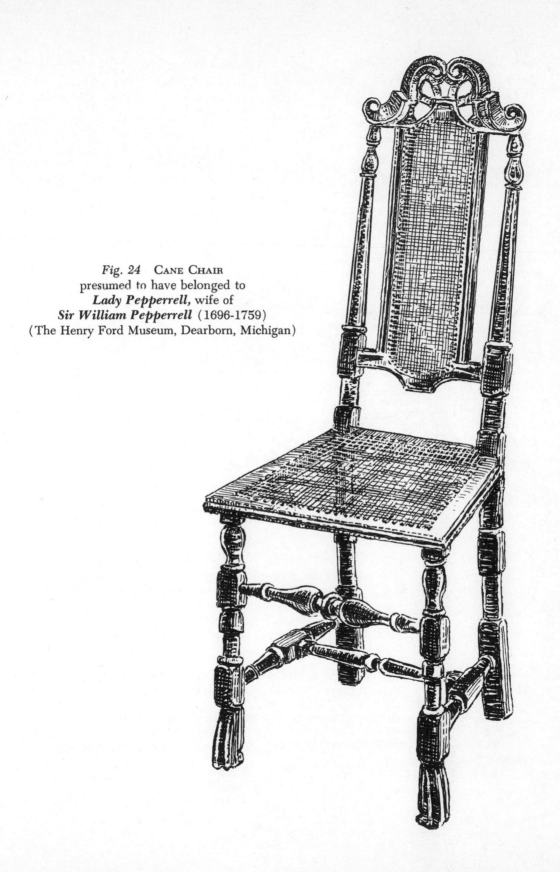

Fig. 24 CANE CHAIR
presumed to have belonged to
Lady Pepperrell, wife of
Sir William Pepperrell (1696-1759)
(The Henry Ford Museum, Dearborn, Michigan)

Fig. 25
The three types of cane chair are identified by their crests:
    First—crest between posts
    Second—crest above posts
    Third—crest formed by arched molding

Cane Chairs of a different figure, and a great chair for a Chamber, all black Walnut."[3]

[1] *Letter-Book of Samuel Sewall* (Collections of the Massachusetts Historical Society), Ser. 6, I, 4, n. 1.

[2] R. W. Symonds, "The English Export Trade in Furniture to Colonial America," Parts I & II, *Antiques,* June, October, 1935.

[3] *Letter-Book,* Ser. 6, II, 106.

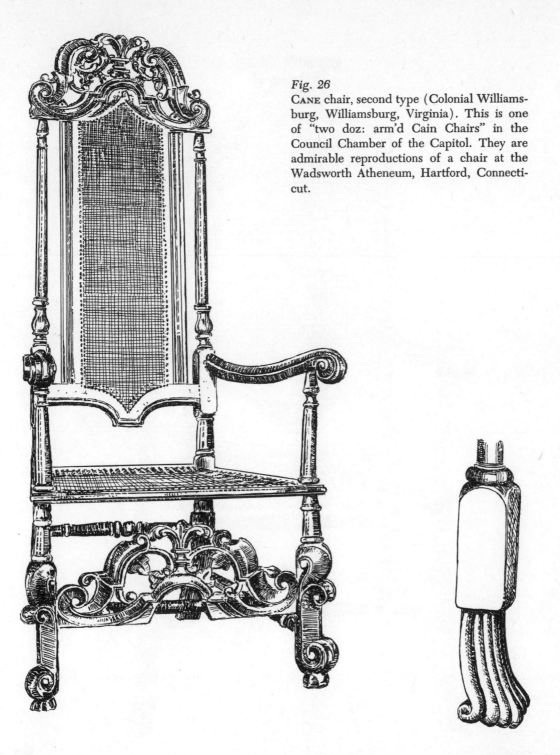

Fig. 26

CANE chair, second type (Colonial Williamsburg, Williamsburg, Virginia). This is one of "two doz: arm'd Cain Chairs" in the Council Chamber of the Capitol. They are admirable reproductions of a chair at the Wadsworth Atheneum, Hartford, Connecticut.

Fig. 27
Spanish foot

Fig. 28
CANE chair, third type, said to have been *William Penn's* (Independence National Historical Park, Philadelphia). Molded wood forms the crest and stiles of the back.

CHAPTER TWO

Turned Chairs of the Eighteenth Century

BANISTER-BACK
SLAT-BACK
WINDSOR

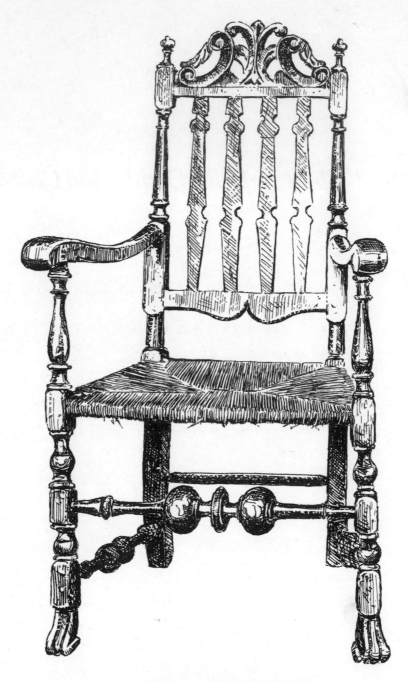

Fig. 29 BANISTER-BACK ARMCHAIR
with a crest like those on cane chairs,
split banisters in the back,
and a ball-and-ring turned front stretcher.
(Wadsworth Atheneum, Hartford, Connecticut
from Nutting's *Furniture Treasury*)

7. *BANISTER-BACK* (*c.* 1700-*c.* 1730)

Maple and other woods

Painted black

> *On Monday the 17th of April . . . there will be exposed to Sale at publick Vendue, on Credit, at the Store-house of David Clarkson over against the Fort, Sundry sorts of European and East India Goods, being the Remainders of several Cargoes, viz: Fine Spanish Cloths, Shalloons, Camblets, Camblet Stuffs, Callimincoes, Durants, English Damasks, Ditto India, China Tafities, plain, striped and flowered Persians, Cherry-derries, Gingrams, Grograms, Sattins, Cheerconnies, Sooseys, Atchabannies, Threads, Mohair, Buttons, Callicoes, Chints, Muslins, Garlicks, Hollands Linnen, Cambricks.*
>
> *The New-York Gazette*
> March 27 – April 3, 1732

THE ships that came from across the seas brought quantities of textiles for the colonists' needs. Some, like chintz and velvet, are familiar to us today, but others, like perpetuana and tamerine, are names that we do not know. Several names had geographic significance; weavers in far-flung localities specialized in particular kinds of cloth which were named after the city of origin. Thus kersey came from Kersey, in Suffolk, England; duffel from Duffel, Belgium; shalloon from Châlons, France; osnaburgh from Osnabrück, Prussia; padusoy from Padua, Italy; calico from Calicut, India; and nankeen from Nanking, China.

Many of the yard goods were used to furnish the dwellings. Tablecloths, napkins and other household linens were plentiful but very costly compared to the furniture. For example, at Newbury, Massachusetts, in 1690, Nathaniel Clarke's "16 payr of sheets" were appraised at £14, while his "2 duzen and 9 chairs" were only a little over £6.

The colonists had "suites" of curtains for beds and curtains for the small casement windows. Their cupboard cloths were for cupboards but, strangely enough, their carpets usually were placed on tables and their rugs on beds. Carpets were not in general use on floors until around 1750. Table carpets were

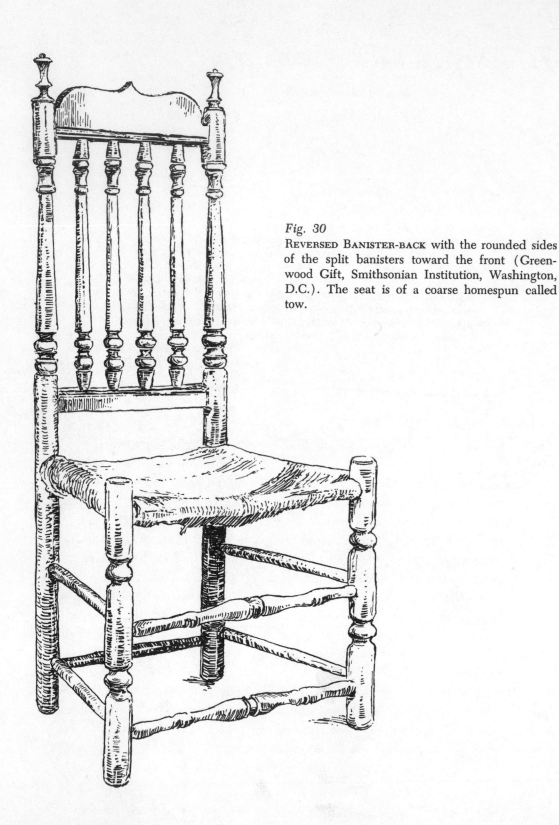

Fig. 30
REVERSED BANISTER-BACK with the rounded sides of the split banisters toward the front (Greenwood Gift, Smithsonian Institution, Washington, D.C.). The seat is of a coarse homespun called tow.

Fig. 31
American craftsmen made crests of their own designs such as:

    a) wild rose   c) sunrise
    b) fish tail   d) scalloped

made of calico, broadcloth or of richer fabrics, or they were oriental "Turkey Carpets." Rugs, frequently of coarse worsted, always were listed with blankets, quilts and other bedding.

Cushions, spelled cooshens, queshions, cussings, and other ways, were numerous. At times they were made of damask, brocade or of other expensive materials, or of needlework such as turkeywork.

Cushions and chairs sometimes were listed together like the "ten quishings and chares" owned by the Reverend Ezekiel Rogers in 1660. This entry was followed by "more quishings" and "buffit, stools and forms."[1] Occasionally cushions were called squabs, especially the long flat ones for window seats or couches. Chairs with cane, rush, splint or wood seats obviously were far more comfortable with cushions. They were placed on banister-back chairs as well as on wainscot, slat-back and other styles already considered.

The banister-back was a simplification of the cane chair. At first it looked much like the cane chair except that banisters, similar to those in a stairway, were substituted for cane in the back, and rush, or less often splint, was used instead of cane in the seat (Fig. 29). This style is also called the baluster-back, since baluster is the earlier and more correct name for the slender spindles that support the stair rail.

The back posts of a banister-back are turned like whole banisters, while those between them are half banisters. The latter are from three to five in number, usually four. Before they were turned, two pieces of wood were glued together with cloth or paper between them. After turning, the banister could be split apart with ease. The flat side of the split banister generally is toward the front of the chair. When the turned side faces the front the chair is called a reversed banister-back (Fig. 30).

The crest of the cane chair was carried over to the first banister-backs, but before long our craftsmen were making crests of their own designs. These had less carving and sometimes only a decorative outline on the upper edge. Either the carving or the outline suggests the names for these crests, such as the wild rose, the sunrise or the fish tail (Fig. 31).

The oft-mentioned couch was a day bed or chaise longue. Cane and banister-back couches were similar to the chairs, except that the backs were short and wide to conform to the wider, elongated seat. The backs of some couches had straps or chains attached to the posts so that the rest of the back could be raised or lowered.

Children's chairs (Fig. 12) and infants' high chairs (Fig. 163) are found in most furniture styles, especially the turned banister-back (Fig. 32), slat-back and windsor. Many are of good design, have admirable turnings and claim particular attention because of the universal affection for childhood.

[1] *Essex County Probate*, I, 334-5.

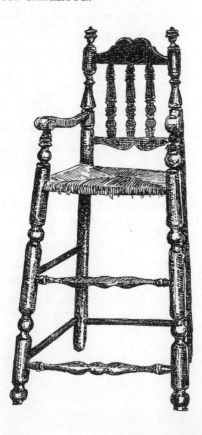

Fig. 32
BANISTER-BACK HIGH CHAIR with good turn-ings (Nutting's *Furniture Treasury*).

8. *BANISTER-BACK* (*c.* 1700-*c.* 1730)

Maple and other woods

Painted black

At the House of the late T. Holton, Chair-maker on the Green, the same business is carried on, where Chairs and Couches are made and mended, after the same manner and at reasonable Rates.

The South Carolina Gazette
(Charleston) August 5, 1732

THE textiles imported by the colonists were in all colors of the rainbow. They liked to wear bright garments as well as somber ones and they chose gay fabrics for their houses. The young wife of John Winthrop, Jr. possessed a "sea greene" gown and a red wool cloak in 1633. Elder Brewster owned a red cap, a green waistcoat and a violet-colored cloak. President Dunster of Harvard had a "yellow Serge mantle," two scarlet mantles and a "red shagged cloake."

This love of colorful dress continued through the years. Judge Sewall sent to London in 1714 for "Red and White Flowerd silk enough to make a Womans Suit" and Benjamin Franklin advertised in 1750 for clothing that had been stolen. Missing were "a woman's long scarlet cloak" and a printed gown, "the ground dark with large red roses and other large red and yellow flowers . . . and smaller blue and white flowers, with many green leaves."

Fabrics in vivid hues added much warmth to the households. Many yards of material were used in the suites of curtains and valances for the canopy beds. A "red wrought suite" was on one of the eleven beds in the home of President Dunster in the 1640's. Another bed had a "very rich and costly" suite of blue serge trimmed with lace and fringe and "a blue Rug to the bed." Another was green "in the same manner," while a fourth had a red coverlet trimmed with green lace.

The red cloth chairs that belonged to William Paine (p. 22) were in a chamber that had a bed with red curtains, "4 red stooles," four other chairs and much other furniture. Occasionally, rooms were referred to by color, like the "yellow roome" and the "red roome" in the manor of Mrs. Elizabeth Digges of Virginia in 1691.

Fig. 33 BANISTER-BACK ARMCHAIR
with crown and heart crest
and reeded banisters.
(Collection of Mrs. Katharine Prentis Murphy,
New-York Historical Society, New York City)

44

Slip covers, then called covers or cases, were made from some of the cloth that was imported.[1] As early as 1653 the several chairs, stools and the couch in the hall of Captain William Tyng of Boston were "all cased" in green. He also had "blew Covers" for the chairs and stools in a chamber that had blue curtains for the bed and windows.[2] Captain George Corwin of nearby Salem had "8 Red . . . chaires wth Covers" in his red chamber in 1684.[3]

Seat cushions added smaller splashes of color to a room. They were particularly effective on chairs painted black such as the banister-back. Turned chairs like the slat-back and banister-back were less formal than joined chairs and also less expensive. This seems to have been recognized at Pennsbury Manor. A "suit of satin curtains" was in the best chamber where there were "sundry" cane chairs, but a "suit of striped linen curtains," was in a chamber that had four rush-bottomed chairs.[4]

As time went on banister-back chairs became more and more simplified. A straight or curved top rail replaced the crest, and the cross rail that the banisters entered just above the seat was often straight rather than shaped on the lower edge. Narrow strips of wood, usually reeded, were substituted for the split banister (Fig. 33). Reeding is a series of ridges carved to look like a cluster of reeds (Fig. 35a).

The arms usually were rolled or turned, and they either extended over the front post (Figs. 29, 32) or entered the front post. On the latter the post sometimes had a ball or mushroom turning like those on seventeenth-century chairs (Fig. 8). Turned chairs of many styles occasionally had an additional spindle under the arm and parallel to it (Figs. 33, 35b). The carved Spanish foot of the cane chair was seen on the first banister-backs, but it gave way to a turned foot, often ball-shaped (Fig. 33), or to no foot at all.

In judging the merit of a turned chair, the finials and turnings are always noted. The finials on eighteenth-century chairs are smaller and less elaborate than those on earlier chairs such as Governor Bradford's, but they should always be observed. Vigorously and deeply turned posts are much more desirable than those that are shallow-turned, and a front stretcher with bold turnings (Figs. 29, 37) adds distinction to any chair.

[1] Marion Day Iverson, "Slipcovers of Past Centuries," *Antiques,* October, 1951.
[2] Suffolk County Probate, II, 138-9.
[3] Dow, *Every Day Life,* p. 276.
[4] Watson, *Annals of Philadelphia,* II, 106.

Fig. 34
BANISTER-BACK with a curved top rail instead of a crest, and good turnings. Narrow strips of reeded wood are substituted for split banisters (Nutting's *Furniture Treasury*).

a

b

Fig. 35
a) reeding—a series of ridges

b) arm with a parallel spindle under it

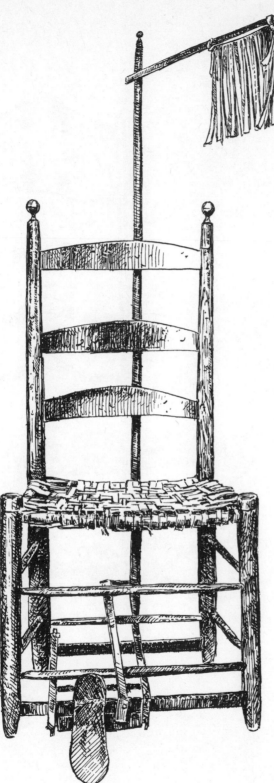

Fig. 36
So-called Sʜᴏᴏ Fʟʏ chair with a
treadle to keep the fly switch overhead in motion (Nutting's *Furniture
Treasury*).

Fig. 37 SLAT-BACK CHAIR
of the Pennsylvania type with
arched slats and exceptional turnings on
the front posts and stretcher.
(Nutting's *Furniture Treasury*)

9. *SLAT-BACK* (*c.* 1630 to the present day)

Maple and other woods

Painted black, red, green

Chairs, of different Sizes, well bottomed with Flag, to be sold at the House of Mr. Seth Sears, in New-London, by Peter Rogers, cheap for Hard Money, Paper Money, West India Goods or Country Produce.

The Connecticut Gazette
and the Universal Intelligencer
(New London) November 28, 1780

BENJAMIN FRANKLIN was seated on the lawn of his Philadelphia home one afternoon in July, 1787, talking to a few fellow members of the Constitutional Convention, when the Reverend Manasseh Cutler stopped by to pay a call. He noticed that Franklin "had an incessant vein of humor, accompanied with an uncommon vivacity" which seemed "as natural and involuntary as breathing."

After tea Franklin showed them his library, including "his great armed chair, with rockers, and a large fan placed over it, with which he fans himself, keeps off flies, etc., while he sits reading, with only a small motion of his foot."[1] Windows were not yet screened and others besides Franklin attached a treadle to a chair so that a fly switch or fan could be put in motion overhead (Fig. 36).

Rockers probably were attached to chairs before Franklin's time. They seem to have been suggested by the cradle, for many early chair rockers were wide and of equal length front and back. Frequently they were added to chairs that were already old, but chairs with posts enlarged to receive the rocker are conceded to have been rocking chairs when they were made. Enlarged posts on what seems to have been a seventeenth-century rocker (Fig. 38) give credence to an earlier date than many suppose.[2]

Americans delighted in contrivances for their chairs. A conical spring placed

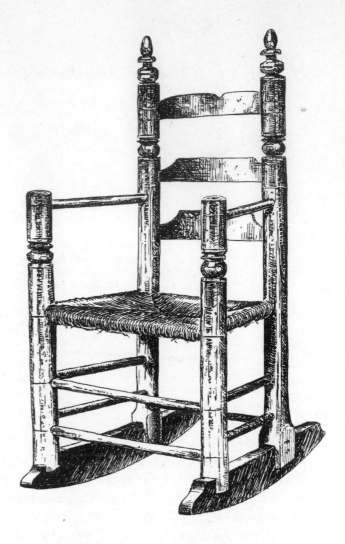

Fig. 38
SLAT-BACK ROCKING CHAIR with heavy posts and elaborate turnings of the 17th century. The back posts are enlarged to receive the rockers ("Home, Sweet Home," East Hampton, Long Island, N.Y.—from Lockwood's *Colonial Furniture in America*).

under each front post gave almost a rocking sensation. Candle holders were hung on the top rail or fitted over the front posts to give better light for reading or hand work. These and other ingenious devices were most often seen on turned chairs, especially on the slat-backs.

The slat-back is the one style of chair known to our first English colonists that has continued in use through the years. Slat-backs of the eighteenth century are lighter in scale than those of the seventeenth. They, like other styles, developed regional characteristics. Slat-back chairs made in Pennsylvania and adjacent colonies are quite unlike the ones made in New England and nearby northern New York. In overlapping areas there was a mingling of the features of both types. Very little is known about the slat-back chairs of the southern colonies.

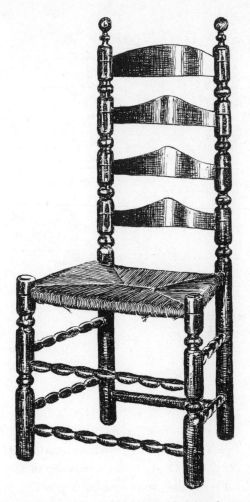

Fig. 39
SLAT-BACK chair of the New England type, with ornamental turnings on the back as well as the front posts, sausage-turned stretchers, and a rush seat (George Dudley Seymour Collection, Connecticut Historical Society, Hartford).

The most distinguishing feature of the so-called Pennsylvania slat-back is the shape of the slat. It has a high arch in the center and often the lower edge is arched as well as the upper edge (Fig. 37). Five and even six slats are found and frequently they are graduated in size, with the widest at the top. Slat-back chairs are spoken of as ladder-backs and also as three-back, four-, five- or six-back chairs, according to the number of slats.

Pennsylvania chairs have ornamental turnings on the front posts only. Often they terminate with a ball foot that is larger than the post above it. The back posts have finials at the top and they taper near the floor. Pennsylvania slat-backs frequently have the desirable large and deeply turned front stretcher.

The slats on New England chairs are likely to be fewer in number and they are not bent outward as much as those on Pennsylvania chairs. Usually the slats

51

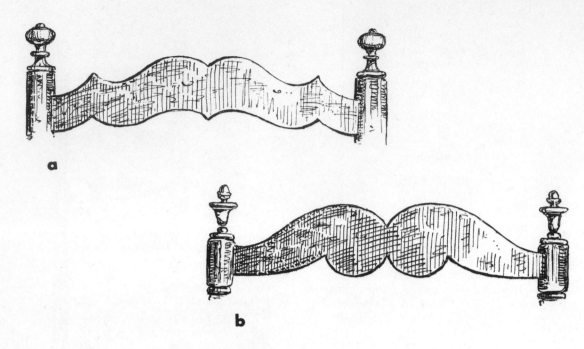

Fig. 40
a) serpentine slat
b) salamander slat

are straight on the lower edge (Fig. 39). Two exceptions are the serpentine and the salamander slats (Fig. 40a-b). The latter is found in France and in the French Canadian provinces and the few in this country have come from northern New England, so they may be of Canadian origin. Decorative turnings are seen on both the front and back posts of New England slat-backs. Those with sausage turned stretchers (Fig. 39) are much sought after.

Slat-back chairs in all of the colonies were painted black, dark red or, occasionally, green. In Pennsylvania, around 1740, they were seen in still other colors and sometimes were "flowerd"—decorated with floral designs.[3]

As far as we know slat-backs were the only chairs with rush seats being made in large numbers at the time of the American Revolution. When Charlestown, Massachusetts, was burned by the British during the battle of Bunker Hill, the brothers Larkin, chairmakers, lost twelve hundred "bundles Flags," certainly enough to bottom a good many chairs.[4]

[1] *Life Journals and Correspondence of Rev. Manasseh Cutler,* I, 269.
[2] Lockwood, *Colonial Furniture,* II, 14-15.
[3] William McPherson Hornor, Jr., *Blue Book of Philadelphia Furniture,* p. 294.
[4] Mabel M. Swan, "Furniture Makers of Charlestown," *Antiques,* October, 1944.

10. *WINDSOR* (*c.* 1720-*c.* 1825)

LOW-BACK
HOOP-BACK
Variety of woods, painted

Made and sold by Josiah Sherald, at the Sign of the Gold-headed Cane, in Second-street, a little below Dock Bridge, All Sorts of Rush-bottom Chairs, Windsor Chairs, Couches, Canes, &C. made in the best Manner, and newest Fashions, which he will sell low for Cash or short Credit . . . The said Sherald will barter Chairs for Goods at Cash Price.

Pennsylvania Gazette
(Philadelphia) September 5, 1765

WHEN John Adams left Quincy, Massachusetts, for the Continental Congress, in 1774, his wife Abigail and their small children stayed at home. In his years of public life that followed they were often separated and their published letters tell us much about the events of their day and reveal some of their problems, such as the irregularity of the mail.

Mrs. Adams once fretted because she had not had "one syllable" from her husband in Philadelphia for more than five weeks. When she received "a fine parcel of letters" she was jubilant. "My heart is as light as a feather and my spirits are dancing." In February, 1778, John Adams and their son, ten-year-old John Quincy, sailed for France and by June Mr. Adams felt "a great deal of anxiety" because he had not "received a line nor heard a word" concerning his wife. Meantime she waited four and a half months for "the first line which has blessed my sight."

In June, 1775, they had written each other momentous news. He told her that "the modest and virtuous, the amiable, generous, and brave George Washington" had been chosen General of the Army. Ten companies were to be sent to Boston, "the most accurate marksmen in the world" because they used "a peculiar kind of musket, called a rifle."

Fig. 41 Hoop-back Windsor
presumed to have belonged to
John Adams (1735-1826)
(John and Abigail Adams Cottage, Quincy, Massachusetts)

At approximately the same time Mrs. Adams wrote him about the battle that began "upon our intrenchments upon Bunker's Hill, Saturday morning about three o'clock, and has not ceased yet, and it is now three o'clock Sabbath afternoon . . . The constant roar of the cannon is so distressing that we cannot eat, drink or sleep."

A windsor chair in the John Adams cottage in Quincy is said to have been his favorite chair, perhaps because the legs were cut off, making it more comfortable for the short statesman (Fig. 41). It is a hoop-back windsor that is believed to have developed from the low-back windsor.

The low-back has a semicircular top rail, often with a raised portion in the center of the back (Fig. 42). This semicircular rail is retained in the hoop-back

Fig. 42
LOW-BACK WINDSORS have a semicircular top rail (Nutting's *Furniture Treasury*). This low-back also has a writing arm and three drawers for writing paraphernalia.

Fig. 43
HOOP-BACK WINDSOR believed to have
been made for Independence Hall in
1778 by Francis Trumble, marked "F. T."
(Independence National Historical Park,
Philadelphia).

and spindles extending above it are enclosed with hoop-shaped wood. Since the
hoop looks something like a bow, it is also called a bow-back. Originally it appears
to have been known as a sack-back, though the reason for this is obscure.

Low-back and sack-back windsors were among those ordered from Francis
Trumble, a Philadelphia chairmaker, for Independence Hall in 1778 (Fig. 43).[1, 2]
The Hall was then being refurnished, after having been used as a prison and
hospital by the British when they occupied the city. The chairs for Independence
Hall had a lower hoop and one more commonly seen than the high hoop on the
John Adams chair.

Windsor chairs are presumed to have been made first in England near the
town and castle of Windsor, but they received their highest development in
America. The English windsor never acquired the lightness and subtle charm of
the American chair. Usually it had a pierced splat at the center of the back
(Fig. 44), while the American chair back was made entirely of turned spindles.

Fig. 44
ENGLISH WINDSORS have a pierced splat
and legs with less rake than on American
chairs (*Antiques,* September, 1949).

Its legs, poorly turned, did not have the decided rake or outward slant of the
legs on our windsors which adds so much to their stability and style.

Legs of English windsors were placed near the edge of the seat, while those
on American chairs were about three inches from the edge. Holes for them were
bored in the seat at an angle to give them the rake without which they would
appear stiff, like those on English chairs.

A single piece of wood, often pine, forms the seat. Usually it is thick and,
when shaped like a saddle, very comfortable. The underside of the seat edges
as a rule are chamfered or cut away, so that the seat does not appear as heavy
as it is (Fig. 50b). The method of making windsors is sometimes spoken of as
"stick" construction. The British refer to them as "stick-back" chairs. In 1809
Thomas Jefferson ordered "3 dozen stick chairs, painted black with a yellow
ring."[3]

[1] David Stockwell, "Windsors in Independence Hall," *Antiques,* September, 1952.
[2] Hornor, *Bluebook,* p. 305.
[3] Marie G. Kimball, *The Furnishings of Monticello,* pp. 5, 10.

Fig. 45 COMB-BACK WINDSOR
presumed to have belonged to
Thomas Jefferson (1743-1826)
(American Philosophical Society, Philadelphia)

11. *WINDSOR* (*c.* 1720-*c.* 1825)

COMB-BACK
FAN-BACK
Variety of woods, painted

Imported from Philadelphia in the Brigantine Philadelphia Packet, Francis Johnson, Master, and to be sold by Sheed and White, at their store in Church Street. A large and neat assortment of Windsor Chairs, made in the best and neatest manner, and well painted, high back'd, low back'd, sack back'd, and settees or double seated, fit for piazzas or gardens, childrens dining and low chairs. Also Walnut of the same construction.

The South Carolina Gazette
(Charleston) June 23, 1766

TALL, red-haired Thomas Jefferson completed his studies at William and Mary College at Williamsburg, Virginia, in 1762. As a student his intellectual qualities were so outstanding that he had been invited to dine once a week with Professor William Small, Attorney George Wythe and the Royal Governor, Francis Fauquier, at the Governor's Palace. They were men of learning and culture and had done much to awaken Jefferson's mind.

In less than a score of years this unusual youth would occupy the palace as governor of the Commonwealth of Virginia, but in 1762 he was absorbed in his plans for the next five years. He was to spend them at his home, studying from early in the morning until late at night. He would read history, literature, ethics and many sciences besides Greek, Roman, Saxon and French law. At the end of the allotted time he felt prepared to seek admission to the bar, his years of study the more noteworthy because others, like Patrick Henry, had become lawyers after only a few weeks or months of preparation.

Jefferson little knew that in his scholarly pursuits he was developing the capacity to write one of the most impressive documents of all time. At thirty-three he could so set forth his own "political creed" in the Declaration of Independence that it would become the creed of all Americans for generations to come.

59

The signing of the Declaration, John Adams wrote Abigail, "ought to be commemorated . . . by solemn acts of devotion to God Almighty" and celebrated "with pomp and parade, with shows, games, sports, guns, bells, bonfires, and illuminations, . . . from this time forward forevermore."

Thomas Jefferson, according to tradition, made the first rough draft of the Declaration of Independence while seated in his comb-back windsor (Fig. 45). Though the chair is of utmost importance historically, it has demerits in style. Jefferson is believed to have had the second seat added so that the chair would revolve. This shortened the legs and detracted from the chair's appearance.

Presumably he also added the writing arm because its supporting spindles are placed in the seat itself, while the spindles supporting the writing arms of most chairs are in one or more extensions of the seat (Fig. 42). Writing arms are usually found on the low-back, bow-back and comb-back windsors. Many have one or more drawers under the arm or seat to hold sand, quills, a penknife to sharpen the quills, wafers and other writing equipment.

The comb-back windsor probably also developed from the low-back, since it has the semicircular rail at arm's height. The slender spindles of the back have a shaped top rail over them and together they give the effect of a comb (Fig. 46). The fan-back windsor has the same top rail but on it the semicircular rail has disappeared (Fig. 47). Besides being curved on the upper edge, the top rail is concave, deeply so in the better chairs.

A good top rail, on a comb-back and fan-back, is only about half an inch wide where the spindles enter it and decreases in thickness almost to a knife edge at the top. The ends of the top rail that extend beyond the spindles are called "ears" and spiral scrolls carved on them are praiseworthy.

The spindles on windsor chairs sometimes have been turned, other times shaved like the spokes of a wheel, and occasionally whittled by hand. Whittled spindles can be easily identified because they have a slight bulge (Figs. 42, 51). The large front spindles under the arms of all types of windsors are ornamentally turned and so are the posts on each side of the back of a fan-back.

A good comb-back, far better than Jefferson's, has admirable turnings (Fig. 46), spirals carved on the ears of the top rail and knuckles carved at the ends of the arms (Fig. 50a). The legs have the blunt arrow foot found on early Philadelphia windsors and the stretchers have the H shape seen on eighteenth-century windsors. The center stretcher is ring-and-ball turned, further proof that it is an early chair.

Fig. 46
COMB-BACK WINDSOR with spirals on the ears of the top rail, knuckles at the ends of the arms, and admirable turnings (Nutting's *Furniture Treasury*). The blunt arrow feet are a mark of early Philadelphia windsors.

Fig. 47
FAN-BACK WINDSORS have a deeply curved top rail like that of a comb-back, but without the semicircular rail at arm's height (Nutting's *Furniture Treasury*).

Fig. 48
FAN-BACK WINDSOR, *c.* 1800, made by Moravians for their church in Old Salem (Winston-Salem, North Carolina). Turnings are much less vigorous on late windsors.

12. *WINDSOR* (*c.* 1720-*c.* 1825)

LOOP-BACK
NEW ENGLAND
Variety of woods, painted

John Kelso, Windsor Chair-Maker, from Philadelphia, at Mr. Hyer's in Broad-Street, next door to the General's, Makes and sells all kinds of Windsor chairs . . . , on the most remarkable terms; and as he served a regular apprenticeship in one of the first shops in that way in Philadelphia, he is persuaded he can supply those who may be kind enough to favour him with their custom, with as well-finish'd, strong and neat work as ever appeared in this city.

The New York Gazette
and the Weekly Mercury
August 8, 1774

AS a young Virginia planter George Washington was hospitable and neighborly and apparently liked nothing better than to have Mount Vernon overflowing with friends and relatives. His diaries abound with entries about guests who "came for dinner and spent the night" or several nights.

After the Revolution the General's hospitality was much imposed upon. He and Mrs. Washington had returned home expecting to "spend the evening of our days in tranquility," but their life was far from tranquil. In 1787 Washington compared Mount Vernon to a "well resorted tavern, as scarcely any strangers who are going from north to south, or from south to north, do not spend a day or two at it." Small wonder that the strangers sometimes found the General "very reserved." In that year of 1787 an average supply of pork was set aside for the family table—nearly thirteen thousand pounds.

By 1789 Washington was again bidding "adieu to Mount Vernon, to private life [such as it was] and to domestic felicity," to become the nation's first President. Upon retiring eight years later, he knew that he could not expect seclusion. He still felt obliged to entertain every arrival, though he complained that at dinner "I rarely miss seeing strange faces come as they say out of respect for me. Pray would not the word curiosity answer as well? And how different this from having a few social friends at a cheerful board!"

63

But there came one eventful day in 1797 when the General could write triumphantly, "Mrs. Washington & myself will do what I believe has not been done within the last twenty years by us, that is to set down to dinner by ourselves."

In the spring of 1796 President Washington purchased two dozen "ovel Back Chairs"[1] and had them sent from Philadelphia to Mount Vernon where they were to be placed on the piazza for guests (Fig. 49). "Ovel Back" windsors are now called loop-back or balloon-back. They are like the hoop-backs, except that they have no semicircular rail and the loop begins at the seat. When the loop-back and fan-back windsors are armchairs, the arms are tenoned onto the back (Fig. 50a).

The legs of the Mount Vernon chairs are turned to simulate bamboo, supposedly because of the Chinese influence that began in America around 1750. Bamboo turnings usually are seen on windsors of the early nineteenth century (Fig. 149), but they were on a writing-arm windsor made in Philadelphia as early as 1763[2] and on Thomas Jefferson's comb-back (Fig. 45).

Many think that all types of the American windsor, save one, originated in or near Philadelphia. The exception is called the New England windsor, even though it was also made elsewhere. It is easily recognized because a single piece of wood forms the top rail and arms (Fig. 51). This continuous line is graceful but fragile and it often breaks at the back of the arm where it is sharply bent upward (Fig. 50b).

Some windsors have braced backs. The two bracing spindles are placed in an extension at the back of the seat (Fig. 50b). Since the number of spindles somewhat determines the merit of a windsor, a chair with nine spindles plus two bracing spindles is held in high regard (Fig. 51).

Paint usually covered the different woods in a single windsor. Green was the favorite color; others were red, yellow and white. "Windsor chairs of all colours" were advertised in Charleston, South Carolina, in 1798.[3] A few windsors had brightly colored leather upholstered seats.[4]

Occasionally windsors were made of walnut or other expensive woods. In 1768 six "cherry tree" windsors were in the hall of the Moffatt-Ladd house in Portsmouth, New Hampshire,* and in 1796 six "elegant" windsor armchairs were a part of the mahogany furniture that Stephen Girard of Philadelphia (p. 159) ordered for a wedding gift.

There is an endless variety of windsor chairs but few are uniformly good. A chair may have several excellent features and a single poor one or vice versa.

Fig. 49 Loop-back or "Ovel" Windsor
presumed to have belonged to
George Washington (1732-1799)
(Mount Vernon, Virginia)

Some craftsmen were skillful in shaping the back, others the seat, still others in turning the legs and placing them at the proper rake.

[1] Hornor, *Bluebook*, p. 303.
[2] J. Stogdell Stokes, "American Windsor Chairs," *Antiques*, April, 1926.
[3] Prime, *Arts and Crafts*, II, 173.
[4] Joe Kindig III, "Upholstered Windsors," *Antiques*, July, 1952.

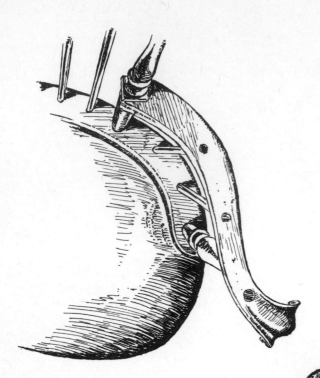

Fig. 50
a) Arm for loop-back and fan-back chairs tenoned onto the back.
b) Bracing spindles placed in an extension of the seat.

a

b

Fig. 51
NEW ENGLAND WINDSOR with top rail
bent to form the arms. It has nine
spindles and two bracing spindles (Old
Sturbridge Village, Sturbridge, Massachusetts).

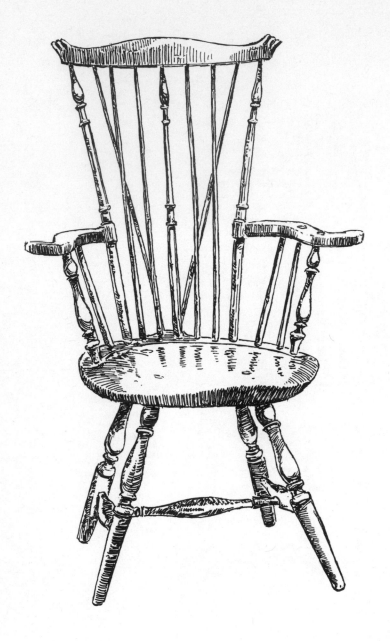

Fig. 52
FAN-BACK WINDSOR with abbreviated top
rail, tenoned arms, and braced back
(Museum of Fine Arts, Boston). This
back is unusual in that the center spindle
matches the posts.

CHAPTER THREE

Chairs of the Early Eighteenth Century

WILLIAM AND MARY

EARLY DUTCH

QUEEN ANNE

Fig. 53 WILLIAM AND MARY UPHOLSTERED ARMCHAIR
one of very few believed to be of
American origin.
(Mrs. J. Stogdell Stokes—from
Nutting's *Furniture Treasury*)

13. *WILLIAM AND MARY* (c. 1700-c. 1720)
EARLY DUTCH (c. 1710-c. 1725)

Variety of woods

> *Run away from Thomas Rigby, of the City of New-York, Joyner, an indented Servant Man named John Howey, about 21 years of Age. He is an Irish Man, and a Joyner by Trade . . . he wears a Wigg, had on when he went away a blew Duffels Coat, Oznebrigs Wast-Coat, and a Pair of Buck-Skin Britches, a Speckl'd Shirt, a new Felt Hat, and a Pair of Yarn Stockings . . . 5 Pounds as a Reward.*
> *The New-York Weekly Journal*
> October 14, 1734

DURING the colonial period of nearly one hundred and seventy years, many places were given the names of English monarchs. Charlestown, Massachusetts, honored Charles I who reigned from 1625 to 1649 while Charleston (originally Charles Town), South Carolina, was named for Charles II who ruled between 1660 and 1685. Jamestown, Virginia, had been settled in 1607 during the time of James I and when the colony decided to move its capital to Middle Plantation in 1699, they renamed it Williamsburg for their sovereign, William III.

In England in 1685 the gay and extravagant Charles II had been followed to the throne by his brother James II. Three years later the unpopular James fled to France when he learned that the soldiers of William of Orange of Holland had landed on British soil. Mary, the wife of William of Orange, was a daughter of James II and soon she and her husband were proclaimed King William III and Queen Mary. In 1693 the college named for William and Mary was founded at Middle Plantation, later Williamsburg, Virginia.

Today Williamsburg appears much as it did two centuries ago because of the restoration begun in the late 1920's by Mr. John D. Rockefeller, Jr. Countless visitors see the capitol and college, the shops and taverns, the dwellings and gardens that again have the beauty and charm of the colonial city.

At the capitol Patrick Henry startled the House of Burgesses and angered the Royal Governor with his fiery speeches. At the college sixteen-year-old George Washington was examined for his surveyor's license. Besides Jefferson, Presidents Monroe and Tyler and Chief Justice Marshall were once students in the same building, designed by Sir Christopher Wren, the English architect.

71

The Royal Governor's pew was quite apart from those of other worshippers in the Bruton Parish church at Williamsburg. It was canopied in silk and had curtains to screen His Excellency from the eyes of the curious and from drafts in the unheated church. An English upholstered chair in the William and Mary style is in the pew today. The legs of this style had the trumpet or the inverted cup turnings. Stretchers were flat, wide and often X-crossed, with a finial at the center. Such a chair is also in the parlor at Pennsbury and is said to have belonged to William Penn.

There is no clearly defined William and Mary style in American chairs, though colonists had William and Mary highboys, tables and other furniture. A high-back upholstered armchair with trumpet turnings, believed to be American, is one of the few that have been found (Fig. 53). The colonists apparently continued to use cane chairs or their counterparts upholstered in leather (Fig. 54). They also used the turned banister-back and slat-back chairs.

Between two furniture styles there often were transition chairs with some features of each style. Soon transition chairs appeared between the cane and the coming Queen Anne style. Cane chairs sometimes had a rudimentary form of the Queen Anne cabriole leg (Fig. 55).

Other transition chairs retained the turned legs and Spanish foot of the cane chair, but the back suggested the Queen Anne (Fig. 56). The yoke-shaped top rail was carved, the vase-shaped splat entered a cross rail above the seat and the seat was of rush. This particular transition chair was made mostly in New England and is called an early Dutch chair.

The Dutch influence had been strengthened in England when Dutch cabinetmakers followed William and Mary to Great Britain. French influence was also being felt because French Huguenot craftsmen had fled to England, Holland, America and other countries for religious protection after the revocation of the Edict of Nantes in 1685.

The word cabinetmaker had begun to replace the word joiner, but joiner was to remain in common usage for several decades. Cabinetmakers who specialized in chairs were becoming known as chairmakers. Judge Samuel Sewall of Boston used the term when he wrote of inspecting "the order of the Town" one night in August, 1715. Among "the players at Nine Pins" he found "Benjamin Davis, Chair Maker."[1]

[1] *Diary of Samuel Sewall* (Collections of the Massachusetts Historical Society), Ser. 5, VII, 51.

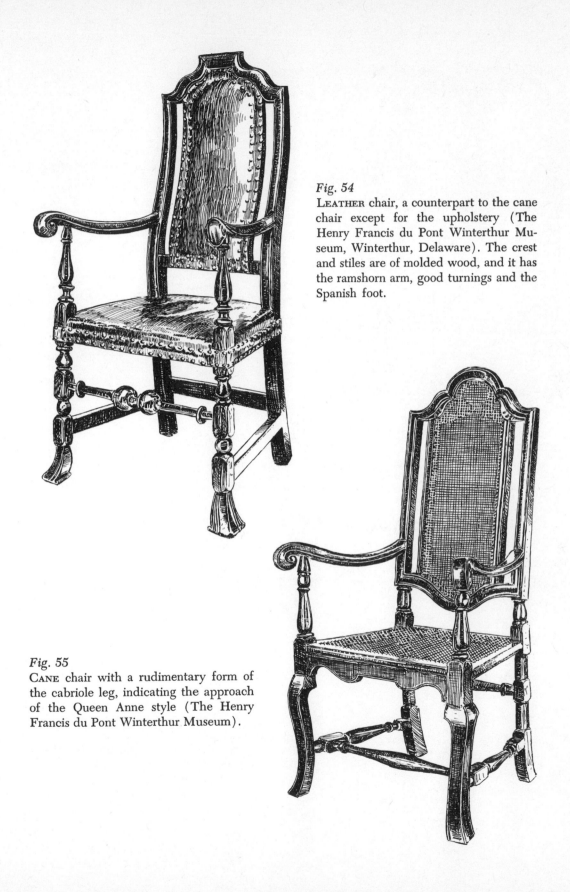

Fig. 54
LEATHER chair, a counterpart to the cane chair except for the upholstery (The Henry Francis du Pont Winterthur Museum, Winterthur, Delaware). The crest and stiles are of molded wood, and it has the ramshorn arm, good turnings and the Spanish foot.

Fig. 55
CANE chair with a rudimentary form of the cabriole leg, indicating the approach of the Queen Anne style (The Henry Francis du Pont Winterthur Museum).

Fig. 56
Early Dutch chair, another transition
chair, with turned legs and the Spanish
foot, but with the back suggesting the
Queen Anne style (The Metropolitan
Museum of Art, New York City).

14. *QUEEN ANNE* (*c.* 1720-*c.* 1760)

Walnut

> *To be sold by Auction, Household Furniture of the late Mr. Pyam Blowers, including . . . Leather-Bottom Chairs, sundry Mehogany and other Tables, a good Couch Squab and Pillow, a very handsome Yellow Damask Bed, an Easy Chair.*
>
> Boston News-Letter
> May 17-24, 1739

PRINCESS ANNE, another daughter of James II, received her share of place names in America both before and after she became Queen Anne in 1702. Virginians named the principal thoroughfare in Williamsburg for her son and heir, the Duke of Gloucester, who did not live to ascend the throne. The college was at one end of Duke of Gloucester Street and the capitol at the other. Between them were private dwellings and public buildings, including Raleigh Tavern.

The Raleigh was a favorite gathering place for old and young. When the governor dissolved the rebellious House of Burgesses in 1769, members reconvened in the Apollo Room of the Raleigh as "the late representatives of the people." Students from William and Mary danced in the Apollo Room and it was there, according to tradition, that they founded the honorary Phi Beta Kappa Society, in 1776. Multitudes gathered when vendues or auctions were held outside the tavern's door. Ships, land, horses and houses were sold there and so were quantities of household furniture.

The governor's residence came to be called the "Palace" after the Burgesses had had to make numerous appropriations for it. When it was finally completed, it became the center of the colony's social life, especially during "Publick Times" when the Burgesses, the Council and the Courts were in session. Then fifty or more guests for dinner appeared to be routine for Lord Botetourt, one of the governors. On the King's Birth-night and other British holidays, the colonial governors gave a ball at the Palace for the "Ladies and Gentlemen" and made provision for the "Populace" to celebrate elsewhere in the city which was "handsomely illuminated" for such occasions.

Today anyone viewing the luxuriously furnished Palace can easily imagine the splendor of the affairs given so long ago. The restored Palace does not have the original furniture, but its inventories were carefully followed when eighteenth-century pieces were selected. They are mostly of English origin because the governors brought their furniture with them. Virginia planters also had English furniture, since they shipped tobacco there and received personal and household needs in return.

Some Queen Anne chairs from Great Britain, such as those in the supper room of the Palace (Fig. 58), were too highly ornamented for the American taste. At that time marquetry, veneer and japanning were in high favor in England. This was seen on some American furniture, but not often on chairs. More to the colonists' liking were the unadorned Queen Anne chairs that had subtle style in their simplicity and in their graceful contours (Fig. 59).

The Queen Anne style was of utmost importance because the predominating lines of furniture now became curved rather than straight. The most marked change was the cabriole leg (Fig. 60a). In Egyptian and other ancient civilizations, furniture had had legs shaped like the legs of animals (Fig. 60b). The French revived this form shortly before it appeared in England on Queen Anne furniture. Possibly they patterned it after the leg of a goat, for the French word *cabriole* means the leap of a goat.

Other curves on the early Queen Anne chair were the yoke-shaped top rail and the vase-shaped splat (Fig. 59). This splat entered the seat, and for the first time the upholstered seat appeared on chairs not otherwise upholstered.

Walnut was the preferred wood, but occasionally cherry, maple or mahogany was chosen in this country. Walnut was not native to England but it was cultivated there. America's first British colonists had been surprised to find it growing in abundance and they soon were exporting it. A century later, apparently, they were still doing so, because "Virginia Wallnut-tree chairs" were advertised in London's *Daily Post* in 1731.[1]

As prosperity came to all of the colonies, the people became more intent upon keeping their dress, their houses and their customs abreast of the mother country. Daniel Neal, a British historian, wrote of New England in 1720: "They affect to be as *English* as possible; there is no fashion in *London*, but in three or four Months is to be seen in Boston."[2]

[1] R. W. Symonds, *Masterpieces of English Furniture and Clocks,* pp. 9-10.
[2] Daniel Neal, *The History of New England,* II, 614.

Fig. 57 Queen Anne Chair
of New England origin
in the Apollo Room of the Raleigh Tavern
Colonial Williamsburg, Williamsburg, Virginia

Fig. 58
ENGLISH QUEEN ANNE chair in the Supper Room of the Governor's Palace at Colonial Williamsburg. Some English chairs were too highly ornamented for American taste.

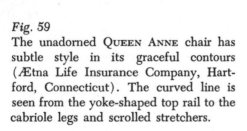

Fig. 59
The unadorned QUEEN ANNE chair has subtle style in its graceful contours (Ætna Life Insurance Company, Hartford, Connecticut). The curved line is seen from the yoke-shaped top rail to the cabriole legs and scrolled stretchers.

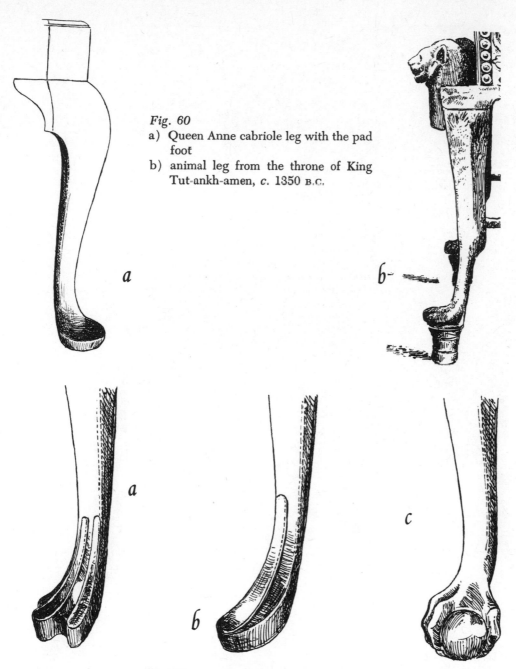

Fig. 60

a) Queen Anne cabriole leg with the pad foot

b) animal leg from the throne of King Tut-ankh-amen, *c.* 1350 B.C.

Fig. 61

The various feet, other than the pad foot, seen on cabriole legs of Queen Anne chairs:

      a) trifid

      b) slipper

      c) claw-and-ball

Fig. 62 QUEEN ANNE EASY CHAIR
presumed to have belonged to
James Logan (1674-1751)
(Mrs. Sarah Logan Starr Blain, Washington, D.C.,
descendant of James Logan)

15. *QUEEN ANNE* (*c.* 1720-*c.* 1760)

Walnut

> *Richard Caulton, Upholsterer, from London, gives this Public Notice
> to all Gentlemen, Ladies, and others . . . He makes and mends Easy-
> Chairs, Dressing Chairs, Windsor Chairs, Settees, Pin Cushion Chair
> Seats, Couches . . .*
>
> *Virginia Gazette*
> (Williamsburg) November 28, 1745

WHEN William Penn made his second voyage to America in 1699, he brought with him twenty-five-year-old James Logan. At half that age Logan had acquired a knowledge of Greek, Latin and Hebrew from his father, a clergyman. After becoming a Quaker, the younger Logan met Penn who was well impressed with his capacities and made him his secretary.

Following the Proprietor's return to England in 1702, Logan acted as his representative in the colony. He also was secretary of the Province for many years and served at different times as mayor of Philadelphia and chief justice and governor of Pennsylvania. Meanwhile he supervised Penn's property and acquired much for himself.

Logan built his country house at Germantown, just outside of Philadelphia, and probably was its architect.* When it was completed, in about 1730, he named it Stenton for the Scotch village where his father had been born. His library, across the front of Stenton on the second floor, contained upwards of three thousand volumes and was an outstanding classical and scientific library for the new country. James Logan was a scholar throughout his life and wrote learned treatises on botany, astronomy and mathematics, often in Latin. Some were printed in Europe, others here, by an enterprising younger Philadelphian named Benjamin Franklin.

In the absence of William Penn it was Logan's responsibility to entertain the Indians. As many as a hundred would arrive at Stenton to confer with him for three days. Once Chief Wingohocking proposed that they exchange names— a distinguished Indian honor. Logan diplomatically suggested that instead the Chief give his name to a creek near Stenton because it would outlive them both.

Fig. 63
Early Easy or Wing chair with crested back and turned leg; the
Spanish foot is partially worn away (The Metropolitan Museum
of Art, New York City). The upholstery is of blue and white
printed linen trimmed with fringe.

In time there were a good many Indians named Logan, but the Wingohocking Creek disappeared.

At Stenton, in 1730, Logan had eleven cane chairs and a couch placed in the back parlor. The "leather bottom'd" chairs in other first floor rooms presumably were in the newer Queen Anne style. Ten chairs with black leather seats were in the front parlor, eight with russet leather in the entrance hall and ten with red leather seats in what seems to have been his dining room.[1]

Some time later Logan acquired an easy chair for his parlor (Fig. 62). This was unusual because they were regarded as bedroom furniture and the seat frame was fitted for a commode. Though often called wing chairs today, they were known to the colonists as easy chairs. The wings kept off drafts, and if the chair faced the fireplace the person sitting in it had a degree of comfort in winter.

Judge Sewall once noted during a Boston snowstorm in 1716, "My ink freezes so that I can hardly write by a good fire in my Wive's Chamber." A Swedish scientist visiting Pennsylvania in 1750 was "forced" to carry his ink in his pocket or to place it on the hearth to keep it from freezing.

There was some variation in the wings of easy chairs and also in the arms. Arms rolled outward horizontally (Fig. 176), or the arm support rolled vertically (Fig. 105), or there was an abbreviated combination of the two rolls with a scroll between that added to their appearance (Fig. 62).

The first easy chairs in America probably had the leg with the Flemish scroll,[2] or the turned leg and Spanish foot (Fig. 63). Many more were made with the cabriole leg of the Queen Anne style. The pad foot was most common on all Queen Anne chairs (Fig. 60a). There was also the trifid foot, called a web foot when it had vertical grooving (Fig. 61a). The slipper foot was slender and pointed and sometimes in Philadelphia was overlaid with a tongue (Fig. 61b). Later the claw-and-ball foot appeared (Fig. 61c). It was of Chinese origin and had come to England from Holland which was carrying on extensive trade with China. According to Chinese lore, it was a bird's claw clutching a pearl.

An upholstered side chair, with a tall back and a low seat, also was at Stenton (Fig. 64). Such chairs are even more rare than the upholstered arm chairs (Fig. 65), and both are museum treasures. Leather, fabrics and needlework, such as crewelwork and needle point, covered chair seats and upholstered chairs. Queen Anne used her needle diligently and set an example to her subjects.

[1] Hornor, *Bluebook*, p. 52.
[2] Alice Winchester, "The Prentis House at the Shelburne Museum," *Antiques*, May, 1957.

Fig. 64
UPHOLSTERED SIDE chair, also called a back stool (The Henry Francis du Pont Winterthur Museum, Winterthur, Delaware). A very rare chair from Stenton, home of *James Logan*; it is upholstered in leather.

Fig. 65
QUEEN ANNE armchair, one of a pair with crewelwork upholstery, originally in a New York home (The Metropolitan Museum of Art).

16. *QUEEN ANNE* (*c.* 1720-*c.* 1760)

Walnut

> *To be sold at publick vendue by Benjamin Church . . . Half a dozen Compass Seat Black Walnut Leather Bottom Chairs new, Mehogany Tables, Feather Beds, etc.*
>
> Boston Gazette
> August 16, 1756

DURING the time of James Logan a Quaker carpenter named Samuel Powel accumulated much Philadelphia property and built some ninety houses. In 1756 he left his son of the same name one of the largest fortunes in Pennsylvania. Three years later it was inherited by his grandson, Samuel Powel III, a student at the College of Philadelphia who was to become one of the most cultivated and discriminating gentlemen in the colonies.

After college he spent seven years in Europe where he was received by Voltaire in France, by the Pope in Italy and by the King in England. While in Italy he traveled with the entourage of the Duke of York. Angelica Kauffman, the artist, became a good friend and his portrait was painted by Benjamin West whom he helped support. In 1760 he witnessed the coronation of George III and reported it "as grand and magnificent a sight as Britain ever beheld." (George I had followed Queen Anne to the throne in 1714 and he had been succeeded by George II in 1727.)

By 1769 Powell was back in Philadelphia, married to Elizabeth Willing, and established in a town house* so exquisite in detail that interiors of two of the rooms have been moved to the Philadelphia and Metropolitan Museums.

Fig. 66 QUEEN ANNE ARMCHAIR
presumed to have belonged to
Samuel Powel III (1738-1793)
(Philadelphia Museum of Art)

Many of our country's founders were guests of Mr. and Mrs. Powel. There John Adams saw "everything to delight the eye and lure the taste." George Washington often had tea, dined or danced at the Powels' and they, in turn, visited Mount Vernon. Both employed the same coachmaker and the Powel coach, believed to be a duplicate of Washington's, is now on exhibition at Mount Vernon.

While he was in Great Britain Samuel Powel III considered buying furniture, but his uncle warned him that Philadelphia joiners might object and, moreover, that their furniture was "as cheap and as well made from English patterns." Many skilled craftsmen were at work in Philadelphia and there the Queen Anne style reached its highest development in America. The artistry of the chairmaker is revealed in the flowing lines of a Queen Anne chair (Fig. 66). Very likely this chair belonged to Samuel Powel II before it went to the third Samuel.

The Queen Anne style continued through the reign of George I and well into the reign of George II, so that late Queen Anne furniture often is called early Georgian. As the style progressed it had more and more curved lines. The cyma curve predominated. Cyma comes from the Greek word meaning wave. Some cyma curves were small, like those at the top of many cabriole legs (Fig. 60a); others were large, like that of the leg itself.

From the side, the back of a Queen Anne chair is shaped like the handle of a spoon, supposedly to conform to the human back. This spooned back actually is a cyma curve. The stiles of late Queen Anne chairs also had a cyma curve (Fig. 67) and the splats were in a variety of curved forms. Arms carried on the rhythm of line. The looped arm favored by the British is seen on the Powel chair. Philadelphia chairmakers often used the so-called Philadelphia arm; cyma curves are particularly noticeable in its arm support (Figs. 59, 73).

Seats, too, became more curved and eventually horseshoe- or bell-shaped. This was originally called a compass seat. A few of the finest chairs had an additional concave curve at the center of the front seat rail (Fig. 66). Queen Anne chairs had slip seats, that is the upholstery slipped inside the seat frame.

American chairs had more carved decoration as the style went on. The shell and the spiral were favorite motifs (Fig. 67). A shell is carved on the seat rail of the Powel chair and also on the top rail where it is flanked by pairs of spirals, each pair forming an S scroll. The splat is veneered to bring out the grain of the walnut, making this one of the few veneered American Queen Anne chairs. Shells usually decorated the knees of cabriole legs, but the acanthus leaves on the knees of the Powel chair herald a motif often used in the approaching Chippendale style.

Fig. 67
PHILADELPHIA QUEEN ANNE chair with curved stiles that also are
rounded rather than flat-surfaced. The seat is bell-shaped (The
Minneapolis Institute of Arts). Spirals and shells are carved on
the top rail and on the knees of the cabriole legs.

Fig. 68

Q<small>UEEN</small> A<small>NNE</small> chair believed to have been owned by **General Joseph Warren** (1741-1775), Boston physician and patriot who fell at Bunker Hill (The Henry Ford Museum, Dearborn, Michigan). Only in New England were stretchers customary on late Queen Anne chairs.

Fig. 69
The back of a Queen Anne chair made
in New York (Museum of the City of
New York). Leaves and a shell are carved
on the top rail. Two horizontal cyma
curves meet at the base of the splat to
form a cupid's bow.

CHAPTER FOUR

Chairs After the Mid-Eighteenth Century

CHIPPENDALE

Fig. 70 CHIPPENDALE CHAIR
presumed to have belonged to
Benjamin Edes (1732-1803)
(*Antiques* Magazine, December, 1925)

17. *CHIPPENDALE* (*c.* 1755-*c.* 1790)

Mahogany

> *To be sold at Public Vendue . . . at the House opposite Mr. Joseph Gale in Sudbury Street . . . a genteel Sett of Mohogony Chairs with Horse hair Bottoms . . . a Crimson Harrateen Bed and Chairs, Several Setts of Chairs.*
>
> Boston Gazette
> June 17, 1765

ON the afternoon of December the 16th, 1773, a "number of gentlemen" met in the parlor of Benjamin Edes, one of the publishers of the *Boston Gazette*. Mr. Edes asked his son Peter to make punch for them and Peter recalled, in a letter to his grandson in 1836, that he filled the bowl "several times." He "was not admitted into their presence," he supposed "for fear . . . of their being known."

The men "remained in the house until dark" when they went to the office of the *Boston Gazette* to don Indian disguise before they dashed off to the wharf to toss tea into Boston Harbor.

Some two and a half eventful years later, in Philadelphia, "a great concourse of people" gathered in the State House Yard to hear John Nixon read the Declaration of Independence for the first time in public. His voice was "clear and distinct" and afterward the cheering crowds pulled down the royal insignia. "Bells rang all day and all night. Even the chimers chimed away." There were parades, "bonfires, impromptu fireworks and other demonstrations of joy. The night was star-light and beautiful."

Shortly before his appearance in the State House Yard, John Nixon had been commanding defenses in Delaware and shortly afterward he was defending New Jersey as a colonel in the Pennsylvania militia. He had been in the shipping business since the age of sixteen when he had inherited Nixon's wharf, on the Delaware, from his father.

In 1780 the credit of Congress was exhausted and the army lacked food and clothing and threatened mutiny. Ninety-two Philadelphians advanced money; Samuel Powel III and John Nixon each subscribed £5000 sterling.

93

Fig. 71
Back of a CHIPPENDALE chair said to have belonged to **Charles Carroll** of Carrollton (Maryland Historical Society, Baltimore). On Chippendale chairs the ends of the top rail are turned down to meet the stiles of the back, as in this case, or they are turned up to form ears, as in Fig. 70.

The Bostonians who whiled away the hours before the Tea Party in the parlor of Benjamin Edes presumably used his Chippendale chairs (Fig. 70).[1] They are characteristically Chippendale, with a curved top rail, pierced splat and generous seat. The top rail of the Edes chair is in the shape of a cupid's bow. The ends of the top rails of Chippendale chairs are either turned up to form ears (Fig. 70) or down to meet the stiles of the back (Fig. 71). The stiles no longer have the curve of those on late Queen Anne chairs.

John Nixon's chair is exhibited in the State House in Philadelphia, now known as Independence Hall. It is a transition chair with features of both the Queen Anne and Chippendale styles. While the top rail, wide back and rectangular seat are Chippendale, the solid splat and trifid foot are Queen Anne (Fig. 72). Another chair is Queen Anne except for its pierced splat (Fig. 73).

Thomas Chippendale, a cabinetmaker, brought out the first English book devoted entirely to furniture designs in 1754. Consequently the style was named for him rather than for the reigning monarch. Chippendale had been baptized at the Otley Parish Church in Yorkshire in 1718. According to some of his descendants, he worked for his father, a joiner, until the ancestors of the Earl of Harewood, noting his skill, offered to establish him in business· in London. Little is known of Chippendale's early years in London, but his marriage to Catherine Redshaw was registered there in 1748.[2]

He seems to have had some standing before his book, *The Gentleman and Cabinet-Maker's Director*, was published, because in the preface he says that

94

Fig. 72

TRANSITION chair believed to have been *John Nixon's* (1733-1808), (Independence National Historical Park, Philadelphia). It has the Chippendale top rail, wide back and generous rectangular seat, and the Queen Anne solid splat and trifid foot.

"persons of distinction" encouraged him in the task. Many of the elite are on the list of over three hundred who subscribed to it before publication. A second edition came out in 1755 and a third seven years later.

In 1755 Chippendale rented for his establishment three houses in St. Martin's Lane, "a handsome and imposing thoroughfare." Twenty-two workmen were noted in a news story of a fire there that same year. Chippendale continued to make furniture, often for the great houses of England, until he succumbed to tuberculosis in 1779. A son, Thomas, carried on the business for a while, but without conspicuous success. When an author described the "extensive premises" in St. Martin's Lane in 1828, he noted that they were "formerly held by Chippendale, the most famous upholsterer and cabinet-maker of his day."[3]

[1] Homer Eaton Keyes, "Another Tea Chair," *Antiques*, December, 1925.
[2] Oliver Brackett, *Thomas Chippendale, A Study of His Life, Work and Influence*, pp. 12-18.
[3] *Ibid.*, p. 103.

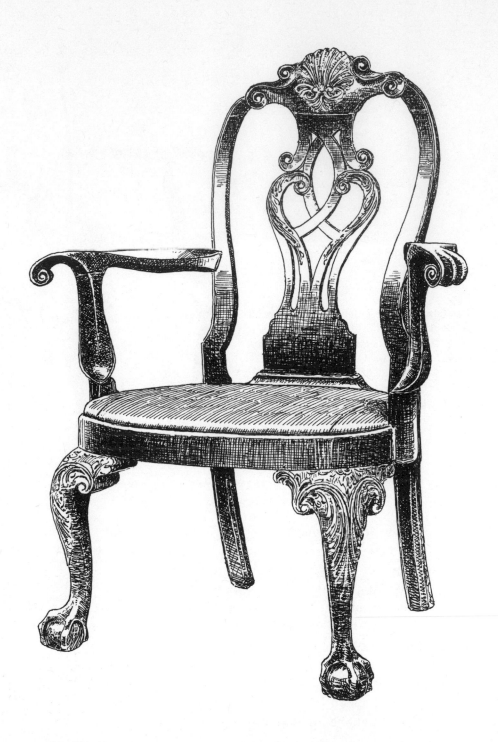

Fig. 73
TRANSITION chair with all the characteristics of the Queen Anne
style, excepting the pierced splat which is Chippendale (The
Metropolitan Museum of Art, New York City). The outcurving
arm with ribbed support was made in Philadelphia (Figs. 59,
104).

18. *CHIPPENDALE* (*c.* 1755-*c.* 1790)

Mahogany

> *Gilbert Ash, in Wall-Street, near the City-Hall, has by him A Parcel of ready made Chairs, Mahogany and Black Walnut, Mahogany Tea Tables and dining Tables, which he will sell, reasonably; Also a Parcel of hard Soap and Candles, which he will sell cheap.*
>
> *The New York Gazette*
> *or the Weekly Post-Boy*
> April 14, 1763

THE Iroquois Indians remained loyal to the English colonies during the French and Indian War, otherwise the French would have had almost certain victory. William Johnson of northern New York was chiefly responsible for their loyalty. He had come to America from Ireland in 1737 to manage his uncle's property in the Mohawk Valley. It was a vantage point for fur trade which Johnson found profitable and the Indians learned that they could rely upon him. He mastered several of their dialects and counseled with them throughout the war.

In 1755 Johnson was commissioned a major general and led the English forces when they routed the French at Lake George. This victory was given particular notice because it followed General Braddock's humiliating defeat in the south. Johnson was soon created a baronet by King George II who also made him sole agent for the Iroquois, otherwise known as the Six Nations.

Sir William, through the years, acquired thousands of acres of land. In about 1762 he built Johnson Hall near Johnstown, New York,* and lived there almost like a feudal lord. He was surrounded by Indian, Negro and white retainers, including a lawyer, a doctor and a school teacher from his native Ireland. He also had an Irish harpist and a violinist to entertain guests who ventured to his pretentious outpost on the American frontier.

His son, Sir John Johnson, inherited the property in 1774. He favored the

Fig. 74 Chippendale Chair
presumed to have belonged to
Sir William Johnson (1715-1774)
(The Minneapolis Institute of Arts)

English during the Revolution and when he learned that General Schuyler had ordered his arrest, he fled to Montreal. Sir John became a colonel with the British army and led raids on the Mohawk Valley. Some time later the New York Assembly confiscated the huge estate.

Sir William Johnson seems to have had a singular fondness for the curved Queen Anne seat, for a set of chairs that he had at Johnson Hall otherwise are completely Chippendale (Fig. 74). In profile view his chairs have the simple curve of Chippendale rather than the spooned back of Queen Anne.

The interlaced scrolls of the splat extend upwards onto the top rail which is handsomely carved. This openwork splat, with a diamond at the center, is identical to one on a chair that was in the Van Rensselaer family which is signed "Made by Gilbert Ash in Wall St. warrented sold April 2, 1756. . . ."[1] Because of the splat and other similarities, Sir William's chairs are also attributed to Gilbert Ash.

Ash and the numerous other colonial cabinetmakers undoubtedly found Chippendale's book of great assistance. *The Gentleman and Cabinet-Maker's Director* was soon followed by books written by Robert Manwaring (pp. 107, 134), Ince and Mayhew and others, but all furniture of that time is now called Chippendale. The books helped to make known the prevailing styles of the mother country and gave instructions to the cabinetmakers. Chippendale gave the exact measurements of most of his chair designs but noted that "sometimes the Dimensions vary according to the Bigness of the Rooms."[2]

Chairmakers in the colonies obviously felt free to vary more than the dimensions. They interpreted British patterns in so many ways that the one hundred and sixty different Chippendale chairs shown in Wallace Nutting's *Furniture Treasury* are only a fraction of what they produced. Our craftsmen were inclined to use less carved ornament than was shown on the English designs, though this was not always true (Fig. 75). American chairmakers understood proportion, scale and beauty of line and their chairs have a distinction quite apart from those made in England (Fig. 76).

Collectors are able not only to differentiate between English and American chairs, but also to decide the approximate locality in which most American chairs were made, as was evident in the Queen Anne style. To acquire this knowledge they study the labeled or signed chairs, such as the Chippendale by Gilbert Ash, or unsigned chairs that are well documented as coming from a definite region. In looking at details of style, construction and carving they find

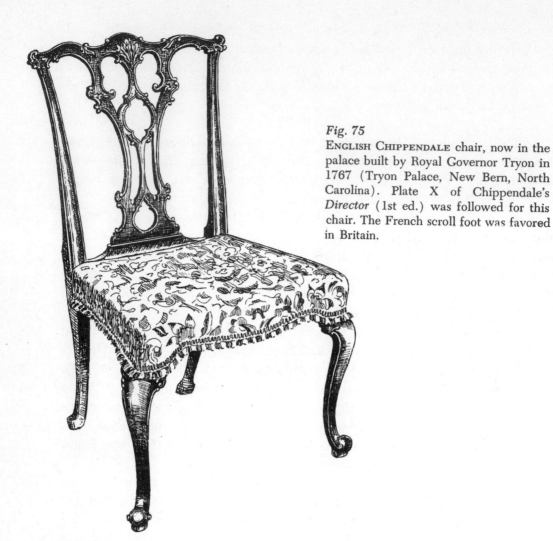

Fig. 75
ENGLISH CHIPPENDALE chair, now in the palace built by Royal Governor Tryon in 1767 (Tryon Palace, New Bern, North Carolina). Plate X of Chippendale's *Director* (1st ed.) was followed for this chair. The French scroll foot was favored in Britain.

many characteristics that distinguish work done in a certain colonial city or even in a particular shop in that city.

Little is known about the furniture made in the early southern colonies although research is in progress (Fig. 77).[3, 4, 5] It has been said that in general New England furniture is "prim," New York's "forthright," and Philadelphia's "urbane."[6]

[1] Homer Eaton Keyes, "A Clue to New York Furniture," *Antiques*, March, 1932.
[2] Thomas Chippendale, *The Gentleman and Cabinet-Maker's Director*, 3rd ed., Pl. XX-XXIII.
[3] "Furniture in the Old South," *Antiques*, 1952.
[4] E. Milby Burton, *Charleston Furniture*.
[5] Samuel and Narcissa Chamberlain, *Southern Interiors of Charleston, South Carolina*.
[6] *Antiques*, April, 1950, p. 288.

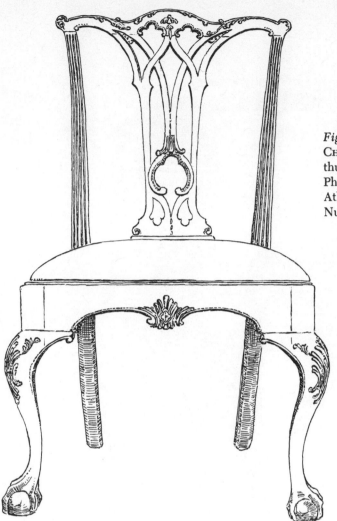

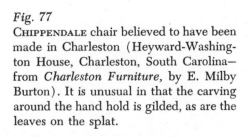

Fig. 76
CHIPPENDALE chair like one at Winter-
thur that has the label of Thomas Tufft,
Philadelphia cabinetmaker (Wadsworth
Atheneum, Hartford, Connecticut—from
Nutting's *Furniture Treasury*).

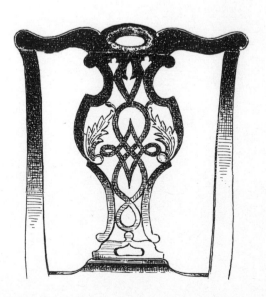

Fig. 77
CHIPPENDALE chair believed to have been
made in Charleston (Heyward-Washington House, Charleston, South Carolina—
from *Charleston Furniture*, by E. Milby
Burton). It is unusual in that the carving
around the hand hold is gilded, as are the
leaves on the splat.

Fig. 78 Chippendale Corner Chair
presumed to have belonged to
Daniel Roberdeau (1727-1795)
(Smithsonian Institution, Washington, D.C.)

19. *CHIPPENDALE* (*c.* 1755-*c.* 1790)

Mahogany

Gerrard Hopkins, son of Samuel, Cabinet and Chair-Maker from Philadelphia at the sign of the Tea Table and chair in Gay Street Baltimore-Town Makes and sells . . . the newest Fashions in Mahogany, Walnut, Cherry-tree and Maple, viz: . . . Chairs of various sorts such as easy, arm Parlour, Chamber or Corner Chairs, Settees, . . .
N. B. Any of the above Articles to be done with or without carved work.

> *The Maryland Gazette*
> (Annapolis) April 9, 1767

ON a September night in 1777 the members of the Continental Congress were aroused from their beds and warned that the British were nearing Philadelphia. They made hasty departures and, after taking circuitous routes to elude the enemy, eventually reassembled in York, Pennsylvania. One of their members, General Daniel Roberdeau, had a house there and invited the Massachusetts delegates to lodge with him. Presently John Adams was reporting to his wife, "General Roberdeau . . . does everything to make us happy. We are highly favored. No other delegates are so well off."

Roberdeau had been elected to Pennsylvania's Provincial Assembly in 1756 and from that time on took an active part in colonial politics. He was a large man, of commanding presence, and was frequently chosen chairman of the mass meetings in the State House Yard. He became brigadier-general of the Pennsylvania militia and both he and Colonel John Nixon fought under General Washington during the New Jersey campaign in the winter of 1776-7.

In the Continental Congress he was especially concerned with economy and honesty in government and made efforts to avoid inflation. When the army needed bullets he offered to develop a lead mine at his own expense and later built Fort Roberdeau to protect it. He was in the merchant trade and outfitted some of his ships as privateers. They brought in valuable prizes. Throughout his residence in Philadelphia he did much for the city's philanthropies, especially the Pennsylvania Hospital.

General Roberdeau was born in the West Indies. His father, a French Huguenot, had found haven there after the revocation of the Edict of Nantes. His mother was a descendant of Scotland's Earl of Glencairn.

General Roberdeau was a "board merchant" and once had a "board yard" at the corner of Cherry and Fourth Streets in Philadelphia.[1] Presumably his "boards" included mahogany since his principal trade was with the West Indies and the finest mahogany came from there. Mahogany not only had beauty of grain and color, but it was easily carved.

Thomas Chippendale scarcely mentioned wood in his *Director*, but his accounts show his frequent use of mahogany. An example is a bill dated 1767 which reads: "10 Mahogany Chairs with neat Open Carv'd Backs the seats stuff'd over the rails, Cover'd with Crimson Haircloth & Brass nail'd."[2] In America mahogany was preferred for the Chippendale style, though walnut and other woods were used.

Mahogany was by no means new in the colonies at the time. As early as 1732 cabinetmakers in Charleston, South Carolina, had advertised "Mahogany Tables and Chairs made after the best manner,"[3] and it was sold at vendue on Boston's "Long Wharffe" in 1737.[4] Mrs. Benjamin Franklin perhaps gave evidence that walnut was no longer fashionable when, in 1765, she relegated their "old black walnut chairs" to a "sleeping room."[5]

The mahogany corner chair said to have belonged to General Roberdeau has the openwork splat of Chippendale chairs (Fig. 78). The first corner chairs, made around 1700, were turned and had the turned or the Spanish foot (Fig. 79). Their seats were of rush. With the coming of the Queen Anne style, corner chairs took on its characteristic solid splat and cabriole legs (Fig. 80).

Corner chairs have a semicircular top rail and its supports usually are turned, but occasionally they are curved (Fig. 80). Those on the Roberdeau chair are turned and stop-fluted. Fluting is a series of vertical grooves and stop fluting is a further refinement (Fig. 84a-b). The deep scallop of the skirt of the Roberdeau chair concealed the commode form.

Sometimes the four legs were all alike, whether cabriole or straight. At other times the front leg was cabriole and the rest were turned, or three were cabriole and the back leg was turned, as on General Roberdeau's chair. Corner chairs were made with and without stretchers, occasionally with the crossed stretcher (Fig. 81).

Fig. 79
Early CORNER chair, turned, with a rush seat, the Spanish foot
in front and the turned foot on the other legs (Heritage Foundation, Deerfield, Massachusetts).

Corner chairs were also called roundabout chairs, or desk or writing chairs, since they were often used at desks. A corner chair with another back above the top rail is known in England as a barber's chair (Fig. 81). Corner chairs are exceptionally comfortable and it is surprising that they were seldom made after the Chippendale period.

[1] Watson, *Annals of Philadelphia*, I, 451.
[2] Brackett, *Thomas Chippendale*, p. 118.
[3] Prime, *Arts and Crafts*, I, 161.
[4] George Francis Dow, *The Arts and Crafts in New England*, p. 129.
[5] Watson, *Annals of Philadelphia*, I, 207.

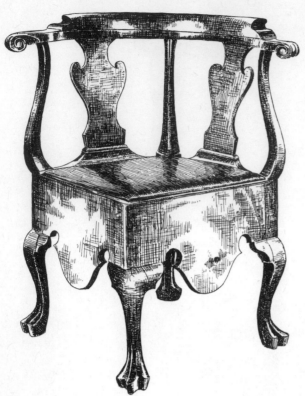

Fig. 80
CORNER chair with the solid splat and
trifid foot of the Queen Anne style (The
Henry Francis du Pont Winterthur Museum, Winterthur, Delaware). The arm
supports are curved instead of turned.

Fig. 81
Dignified CORNER chair said to have been
used by *Governor William Pitkin* of
Connecticut before 1765 (Morgan B.
Brainard, Hartford, Connecticut). It has
an additional back above the usual semicircular top rail; the stretchers are
crossed.

20. *CHIPPENDALE* (c. 1755–c. 1790)

Mahogany

> *Cox and Berry . . . opposite the Rev.* Mr. Cooper's *Meeting-House . . . modern Books of all kinds . . .*
> The Cabinet and Chair-Makers real Friend and Companion,* *containing upwards of 100 new and beautiful Designs of all sorts of Chairs.*
> *Crunden's* Joiner and Cabinet-Makers Darling . . .
> *Barretti's new* Book of Ornaments *very useful for Cabinet-Makers, Carvers, Painters, Engravers, Chasers, &C.*
>
> Boston News-Letter
January 1, 1767
>
> * by Robert Manwaring.

EARLY in 1777 General Washington appointed Elias Boudinot to be the Commissary General of Prisoners. He was an attorney in Elizabeth, New Jersey,* of French Huguenot descent. His responsibilities included supplying food, clothing and blankets to captive American soldiers because British provisions for them were "very small & very indifferent."

Congress did not give Boudinot the necessary "hard money" and he used his own funds and borrowed more on personal credit. In all he spent nearly $30,000, but General Washington promised to meet half of his losses if Congress did not reimburse him. After he became a member of Congress the amount was appropriated reluctantly. Meanwhile, British officers, with whom Boudinot met to arrange the exchange of prisoners, offered him a dukedom or an annual pension of £10,000 sterling if he could "heal the unhappy difference" between the colonies and England.

In 1782 Boudinot was chosen President of Congress, a position comparable to the Presidency today. He signed the treaty of peace with Great Britain and other historic documents. In 1789 he gave a reception at his home in Elizabeth for George Washington who was en route to his first inauguration. Boudinot then accompanied his guest to New York City.

Yale gave Elias Boudinot an honorary LL.D. degree and for forty-nine years he was a trustee of Princeton where two of his fellowships continue. He was always public spirited and many schools, foreign missions and church organizations benefited from his will. In addition, Jews in New York were granted property, Indians were educated and "poor foreigners" were admitted to a hospital

107

Fig. 82 CHIPPENDALE CHAIR
presumed to have belonged to
Elias Boudinot (1740-1821)
(The Henry Francis du Pont Winterthur Museum,
Winterthur, Delaware)

in Philadelphia. That city was left 13,000 acres of "fine wood land of chestnut timber" to provide fuel for its needy.

When Elias Boudinot was elected President of Congress in 1782 he wrote his wife asking her to hasten to Philadelphia. "I have 30 Gent^m to dine with me today—what a figure I cut alone." Besides certain of their servants, she was to bring furniture and silver, since the President's house was "very indifferently furnished." Whether their tassel-back Chippendale chairs were taken to Philadelphia is not known (Fig. 82).

The tassel is carved at the center of the splat of the Boudinot chair, with an acanthus leaf on either side. The acanthus leaf is also seen on the knees of the cabriole legs. After its brief appearance on late Queen Anne chairs it became the leading motif of the Chippendale style. The acanthus grows on the shores of the Mediterranean and was used as a decorative motif by the Greeks and the Romans, notably when they carved it on the capitals of Corinthian columns.

Even though our craftsmen tended to simplify English patterns, there were many richly carved American Chippendale chairs. One of them, another tassel-back, had a variety of motifs in addition to the tassel and the acanthus. There was the shell, scroll, gadroon molding, and stop fluting (Fig. 83).

On the more profusely carved American chairs we sometimes find the paw foot or the scroll foot (Fig. 85a-b), both from Chippendale's designs, the latter of French origin. The claw-and-ball foot remained in favor here, though Chippendale showed it but once in the *Director*—on the posts of a bed.

Chairs were priced according to the amount of carving. Benjamin Lehman of Philadelphia asked so much for "claw feet," more for "shells on the Knees & Front Rail" and still more for "Leaves on the Knees."[1] The chairmaker seldom did his own carving. He either employed carvers in his shop or sent his work to the establishment of a carver. Carvers also were known to employ chairmakers.

Either type of craftsman acquired his skill only after years of work as an apprentice, then as a journeyman under the watchful eye of his master. In time he might have the ability to produce his own masterpiece which would qualify him for the title of master craftsman. From then on the chairs that he made or carved would reflect his particular artistic and creative talents. This individuality of the maker was lost with the coming of factory production in the nineteenth century. The surviving furniture that reveals the genius and the competence of the colonial master craftsmen is justly treasured today.

[1] Harrold E. Gillingham, "A Philadelphia Cabinetmaker and His Price List," *Antiques*, September, 1930, pp. 246-50.

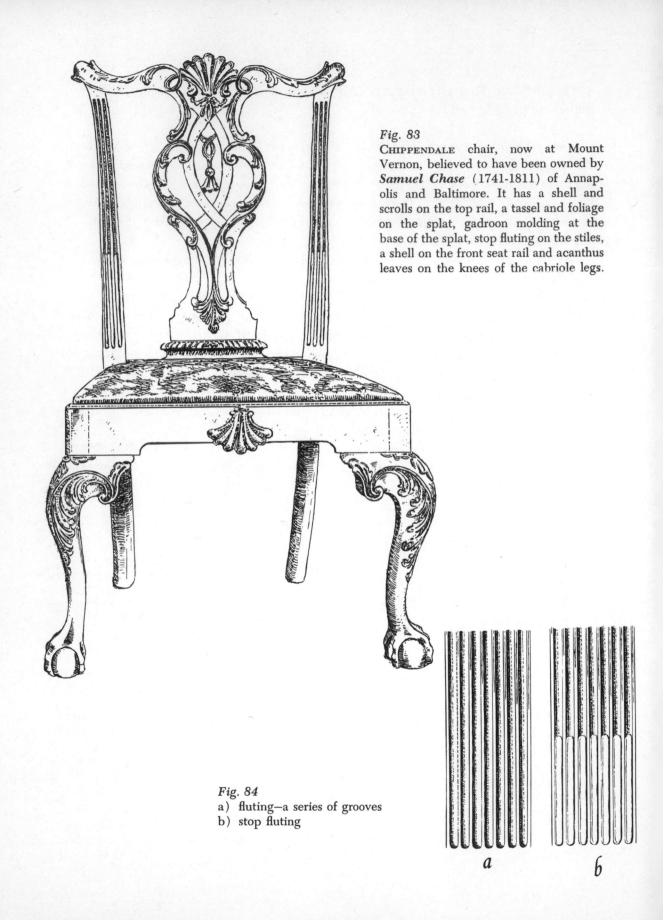

Fig. 83

CHIPPENDALE chair, now at Mount Vernon, believed to have been owned by **Samuel Chase** (1741-1811) of Annapolis and Baltimore. It has a shell and scrolls on the top rail, a tassel and foliage on the splat, gadroon molding at the base of the splat, stop fluting on the stiles, a shell on the front seat rail and acanthus leaves on the knees of the cabriole legs.

Fig. 84
a) fluting—a series of grooves
b) stop fluting

a *b*

Fig. 85
Chippendale cabriole legs usually had the claw-and-ball foot, or occasionally the
    a) paw foot
    b) scroll foot

a

b

Fig. 86
A graceful Chippendale chair back with delicacy in its carving (Mount Vernon).

Fig. 87 CHIPPENDALE LADDER-BACK ARMCHAIR
presumed to have belonged to
William Paca (1740-1799)
(Maryland Historical Society, Baltimore)

21. CHIPPENDALE (c. 1755-c. 1790)

Mahogany

> Joseph Cox, Upholsterer, Cabinet and Chair Maker from London, at the Royal Bed and Star, in Wall-street, New York, Makes all sorts of . . . sopha, settees, couches, burgairs, French elbow, easy and corner chairs; back stools, mewses, ribband back, gothic and rail back [ladder-back?] chairs.
>
> Rivington's New-York Gazetteer
> (Supplement) October 7, 1773

WILLIAM PACA, signer of the Declaration of Independence, came from Harford County, Maryland, where his ancestors, believed to have been of Italian parentage, settled in the seventeenth century. Paca received his Master's degree from the College of Philadelphia in 1759 and afterward went to London to read law in Inner Temple. He returned to practice law in Annapolis and later became a jurist of distinction in both Maryland and Federal courts.

Paca and his wife, the former Mary Chew, had means. Paca spent thousands of dollars outfitting soldiers during the Revolution. When they were discharged he also concerned himself with their welfare. In consequence he was made an honorary member of the Society of Cincinnati, the organization of officers of the Revolution.

Meanwhile Paca was participating in Maryland politics and was twice elected governor. He had been in the Maryland Assembly when the old State House was called "an emblem of public poverty" and he was on the committee responsible for the new State House, built at Annapolis in 1772, which is still in use.* Its senate chamber was one of the meeting places of the Continental Congress, and it was there that Washington resigned his commission on December 23, 1783. From the balcony Mrs. Washington and the wives of other dignitaries watched the stirring event below.

The General and Mrs. Washington had been much feted after their arrival four days previously. Among the affairs was a dinner and ball given by the Continental Congress. Following the official ceremony the Washingtons departed immediately so that they could arrive at Mount Vernon on Christmas Eve. They were escorted some distance on their homeward journey by Governor William Paca and his suite.

When the senate chamber was made ready for the momentous occasion, Governor Paca had additional chairs brought from his Annapolis town house.* Whether his armchair, now exhibited at the Maryland Historical Society, was among them is not recorded. It is a Chippendale ladder-back and has delicate carving on the top rail (Fig. 87). Curiously, each crosswise slat is of different shape, instead of all being alike as on most chairs (Fig. 88). Various pierced designs were seen on this type of chair and the so-called pretzel pattern was widely used (Fig. 89). Though Chippendale did not show ladder-back chairs in the *Director,* like all chairs made at the time they are called Chippendale.

The subtitle of the *Director* gives the source of some of the designs. It reads in part: *Household Furniture in the Gothic, Chinese and Modern Taste.* Great Britain was experiencing a revival of interest in Gothic architecture and Chippendale kept abreast of every trend. Some of his chair backs filled with large Gothic arches cannot be admired, but the Gothic arch did become a more aesthetic design when it was used within a pierced splat (Fig. 90). American chairmakers made adaptations of Chippendale's Gothic patterns (Figs. 71, 109).

Gothic arches are seen in the splat of the Speaker's chair at Independence Hall (Fig. 91). At arm's level, are three trefoils, the Gothic symbol of the Trinity. The Speaker's chair was designed and made for the Continental Congress in 1779 by John Folwell of Philadelphia. Wheat, cornucopias and other symbolic figures were carved on the back. When the Constitution of the United States was signed in 1787, the elderly and frail Benjamin Franklin remarked of the sun carved on the top rail, "Now, at length, I have the happiness to know that it is a rising, and not a setting sun."

John Folwell narrowly missed far greater recognition for his talents. In June 1775 he was ready to publish a book of furniture designs called *The Gentleman and Cabinet-Maker's Assistant.* A proposal signed by several, including booksellers in Philadelphia, Charleston, Annapolis, Baltimore and New York, stated that two hundred drawings "by the ingenious John Folwell" would "be engraved and put to press" as soon as there were three hundred subscribers.[1] It is assumed that Folwell's project was abandoned when news of Bunker Hill reached Philadelphia. Apparently it was the only attempt to bring out a book of American furniture designs of that period and its failure was an immeasurable loss. There is a remote possibility that some of Folwell's unpublished drawings may still come to light.

[1] R. T. H. Halsey and Elizabeth Tower, *The Homes of Our Ancestors,* p. 247.

Fig. 88
CHIPPENDALE LADDER BACK with slats
that have undulating curves (Ætna Life
Insurance Company, Hartford, Connecticut). As is usual, the slats are all of the
same design; **Governor Paca's** chair
(Fig. 87) is surprising in that the three
slats are of different shapes and pierced
patterns.

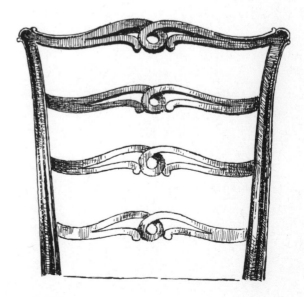

Fig. 89
The pierced design in these slats gives
the chair the name of pretzel-back (Ætna
Life Insurance Company).

115

Fig. 90
One of Chippendale's designs in the Gothic taste, with the Gothic arch in the pierced splat (Pl. XIV, *The Gentleman and Cabinet-Maker's Director*, 3rd ed.).

Fig. 91
Speaker's chair at Independence Hall, made in 1779, with Gothic arches in the splat, three Gothic trefoils below them, and Franklin's "rising sun" carved on the top rail (Independence National Historical Park, Philadelphia).

22. CHIPPENDALE (c. 1755-c. 1790)

Mahogany

AN affluent South Carolina planter named Henry Middleton was president of the First Continental Congress. He did not feel that the colonies should separate from Britain, and when he realized that this would be the will of Congress he resigned, early in 1776. His son, Arthur, became a member in his place and arrived in time to sign the Declaration of Independence.

It is a little unexpected to find Arthur Middleton taking so much opposition to British rule. At the age of eleven he had gone to England for his schooling and he remained there until he was twenty-one. The following year, 1764, he married Mary Izard and later they returned to London where their son Henry was born. A portrait of the small family was painted by Benjamin West. They lived in England and Italy until 1771.

Middleton was on Charleston's secret committee of five that decided to seize the Powder Magazine* there. He joined the militia, was taken prisoner while defending the city against the British in 1780, and was held in St. Augustine, Florida, for a year before his exchange. Following this, he again took his seat in the Continental Congress.

At war's end Middleton turned his attention to repairing the damages the enemy had inflicted on his several plantations, Middleton Place on the Ashley River among them.* His father had begun its extensive gardens in 1741 and, according to tradition, a hundred slaves worked ten years to perfect the plans made by an English landscape artist. Arthur Middleton's son later planted the camellias (the first on the continent) and his grandson the azaleas which add so much today to Middleton Place.

Fig. 92 CHIPPENDALE ARMCHAIR
presumed to have belonged to
Arthur Middleton (1742-1787)
(Nutting's *Furniture Treasury*)

A chair said to have been Arthur Middleton's is of Philadelphia origin (Fig. 92). It has an interlaced top rail and splat and foliage is lightly carved on both. Chairs with similar backs, but with pendant garlands carved on the stiles (Fig. 93), are seen at Stenton and at the Henry Francis du Pont Winterthur Museum. The Middleton chair has the unassuming Chinese lozenge motif carved on the stiles, arm supports and legs. It is one of the motifs found on Chippendale's designs in the Chinese taste.

Interest in Chinese architecture and decoration had been intensified in England around the middle of the century and it soon reached our shores. William Paca had Chinese fretwork rather than banisters in the stairways of his town house.* The earliest Chinese interior in the colonies was at Gunston Hall,* the home of George Mason of Virginia. Colonists liked Chinese wallpaper and selected fabrics, silver, porcelain and other furnishings with Chinese motifs.

Chippendale became particularly enamored of Chinese design but his furniture patterns were not always praiseworthy. The term Chinese Chippendale is heard more often than is justified, perhaps because of the alliteration. His chair backs of fretwork, reminiscent of the Chinese pagoda (Fig. 94), are not held in high esteem and seldom were made in America.

Yet there were elements from Chinese designs, such as the lozenge motif, that Chippendale adapted effectively. Graceful brackets between the seat rails and legs were of Chinese inspiration (Figs. 95, 108). Both Chinese and Gothic fretwork enhanced many parts of Chippendale furniture, including the straight legs of chairs (Figs. 91, 96c).

Occasionally chair patterns in the *Director* have one straight and one cabriole leg, indicating that either would be acceptable. Some straight legs were plain, or had only a beveled edge, others were molded or carved. Still others had a block foot (Fig. 96a-d) and a few of the finest chairs had both carving and the block foot. For some obscure reason the straight leg was called, in Philadelphia, the Marlborough leg.

The slip seat was preferred in this country (Fig. 95), but, Chippendale wrote, "The seats look best when stuffed over the Rails . . . commonly done with Brass Nails in one or two Rows" (Fig. 92).[1] The seat on the Paca chair (Fig. 87) is concave and may be like those advertised by Richard McGrath of Charleston, South Carolina, in 1772. He was making "Hollow-seated chairs . . . which have a light airy look, and make the sitting easy beyond expression."[2]

[1] Chippendale, *The Gentleman and Cabinet-Maker's Director*, 3rd ed., Pl. IX-XVI.
[2] Prime, *Arts and Crafts*, I, 176.

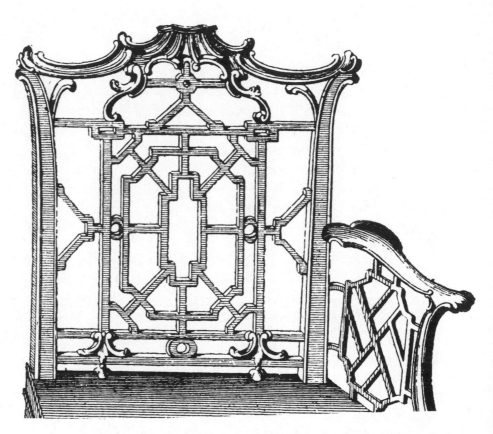

Fig. 93
Pendant garlands on the stiles of chairs with backs similar to the Middleton chair (Fig. 92), (*Antiques*, April, 1955).

Fig. 94
A Chippendale design for a chair in the Chinese taste (Pl. XXVII, *The Gentleman and Cabinet-Maker's Director*, 3rd ed.), with a pagodalike top rail and fretwork filling the back.

Fig. 95
This chair and an English chair (Fig. 75) closely follow some of Chippendale's patterns (The Henry Francis du Pont Winterthur Museum, Winterthur, Delaware). The Chinese lozenge motif on the stiles is also found on the stiles, arms and legs of the Middleton chair.

Fig. 96
Chippendale straight or Marlborough legs:
    a) plain with beveled edge
    b) molded
    c) carved with fretwork
    d) block foot

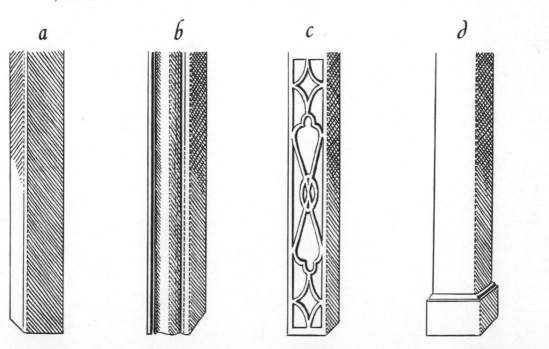

     a   *b*   *c*   *d*

Fig. 97 CHIPPENDALE CHAIR
that bears the label of
Benjamin Randolph (-1791)
(Karolik Collection, Museum of Fine Arts, Boston)

23. *CHIPPENDALE* (*c.* 1755-*c.* 1790)

Mahogany

> *John Lord, Carver and Gilder, . . . at his shop in Meeting-Street;*
> *where gilding, and all the branches of house and furniture carving, in*
> *the Chinese, French and Gothic Tastes, are performed, and flatters*
> *himself, . . . to be capable of executing any ornaments in the above*
> *tastes, to the satisfaction of those gentlemen and ladies who please to*
> *employ him.*
>
> *South Carolina Gazette & Country Journal*
> (Charleston) May 12, 1767

BENJAMIN RANDOLPH of Philadelphia was an ardent patriot as well as a gifted cabinetmaker. His shop was "At the Sign of the Golden Eagle in Chestnut Street" and, as was customary, he lived at the same address. In 1774 he was one of the twenty-eight men who formed the Philadelphia City Troop, still in existence. Each member furnished his own uniform, horse and equipment. The troop was called upon to escort prisoners or to carry money and dispatches, and they crossed the Delaware with General Washington on Christmas Night, 1776.

Thomas Jefferson lodged with Randolph when he came to the Continental Congress in June 1775 and again the following September and May. Jefferson had drawn plans for a small portable desk and asked Randolph to construct it for him. This was the desk on which the Declaration of Independence was written.

In the spring of 1777 Mrs. Washington stayed with the Randolphs en route to her husband's headquarters in Morristown, New Jersey. On May 3rd the General wrote an aide: "Mrs. Washington . . . begs that you inquire what she has to pay at Mr. Randolph's (in Chestnut Street) for the night or two she was there on her way up, and pay it."

Soon the cabinetmaker himself was at headquarters, for Washington sent a letter to Congress on May 11, 1777, "by Mr. Randolph of Chestnut Street." By November, 1778, Randolph had decided to close his shop. He took down the sign of the "Golden Eagle" and advertised furniture, mahogany and "A Quantity of Carvers and Cabinet-Makers Tools . . . for sale at public vendue."[1]

The label of Benjamin Randolph is on a Chippendale chair in the distinguished Karolik Collection in the Boston Museum of Fine Arts (Fig. 97). It is a sophisticated chair, with refinement in line and restraint in ornament.

Curiously, Randolph also is presumed to be the maker of another chair which is the most notable exception to American restraint (Fig. 98). It is one of six chairs, called sample chairs, said to have been made in his shop, though there is no definite proof. All of the six chairs were located in the possession of descendants of Randolph's stepchildren.[2] No two are alike and one is an easy chair. Five are richly carved and since their workmanship is unexcelled, they have brought unprecedented prices when they have changed ownership.

The ornate carved decoration is in what Chippendale called "Modern Taste" in the subtitle of the *Director*. In the German edition of the *Director* "Modern" was changed to "Rococo." When he brought out his third edition he omitted "Gothic, Chinese and Modern Taste" altogether and substituted "the most Fashionable Taste."

The modern or rococo taste was the exuberant French decoration that imitated masses of rocks, shells, foliage, scrolls and other motifs (Fig. 98). Rococo comes from the French words *roc* (rock) and *coquille* (shell). Chippendale boasted that his French-inspired ribband-back chairs were "the best" that he had ever seen, but chair backs with bowknots and streamers of wavy ribbon were never in demand here (Fig. 99).

Our craftsmen used shorter lengths of wavy ribbon (Fig. 100) and modified the rococo in many other ways. Sometimes they combined the rococo with the Gothic or with the Chinese, or even with both, as Mr. Joseph Downs pointed out in his authoritative book on the Queen Anne and Chippendale furniture at the Henry Francis du Pont Winterthur Museum near Wilmington, Delaware.[3] There one finds a Randolph sample chair, the Logan (Fig. 64), Johnson (Fig. 74), Boudinot (Fig. 82), Penn (Fig. 103) and a host of other chairs.

For more than a third of a century Mr. du Pont has been bringing together his unrivaled collection of American furniture, along with ceramics and silver, paintings, fabrics, and other furnishings, all dating from between 1640 and 1840.[4] He has arranged them, with infinitely good taste and with unusual awareness of color, in over one hundred rooms, each from a dwelling of long ago. Winterthur has been opened to a limited number of daily visitors whose great privilege it is to see this unbelievable array of rare craftsmanship.

[1] Prime, *Arts and Crafts*, I, 224.
[2] S. W. Woodhouse, "Benjamin Randolph of Philadelphia," *Antiques*, May, 1927.
[3] Joseph Downs, *American Furniture, Queen Anne and Chippendale Periods*, No. 141.
[4] "Winterthur Museum," *Antiques*, November, 1952.

Fig. 98
Rococo ornament at its height. This is the most elaborately carved chair believed to have been made by American craftsmen, one of the six so-called Randolph sample chairs (Nutting's *Furniture Treasury*).

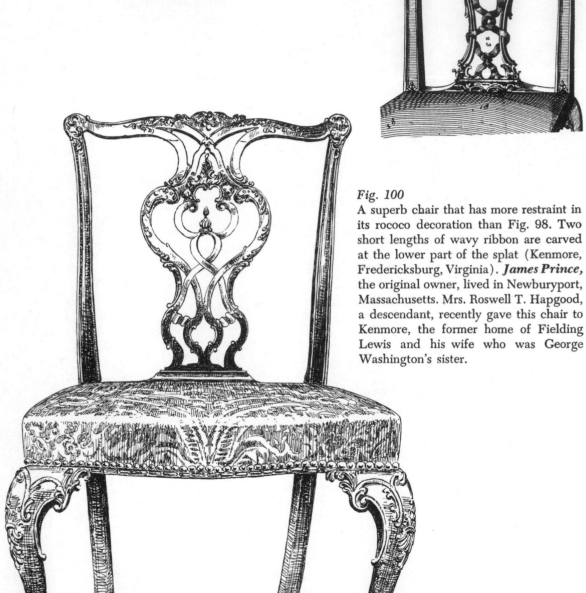

Fig. 99
Chippendale's design for an ornate rib-band-back chair. Such patterns were not often copied in this country (Pl. XV, *The Gentleman and Cabinet-Maker's Director,* 3rd ed.).

Fig. 100
A superb chair that has more restraint in its rococo decoration than Fig. 98. Two short lengths of wavy ribbon are carved at the lower part of the splat (Kenmore, Fredericksburg, Virginia). *James Prince,* the original owner, lived in Newburyport, Massachusetts. Mrs. Roswell T. Hapgood, a descendant, recently gave this chair to Kenmore, the former home of Fielding Lewis and his wife who was George Washington's sister.

24. CHIPPENDALE (c. 1755-c. 1790)

Mahogany

To be sold by William Martin, Upholsterer, next door to the City Vendue-store, in Front-street, Philadelphia.

Part of his stock and Household Furniture, consisting of twelve stuffed-back and seat chairs, three sofas and three easy chairs in canvas, six mahogany Gothic back chairs covered with hair cloth and brass nailed, one French elbow ditto.

Pennsylvania Packet
(Philadelphia) March 13, 1775

THE gentlemen of pre-Revolutionary America, for all their attention to business and politics, often gave the last word about the interior decoration of their homes. While Benjamin Franklin was in England leading the colonies' opposition to taxation, his family moved into their new house. Mrs. Franklin wrote him every detail, even where she had hung "brother John's picture, and one of the King and Queen."

In the blue room there was "the harpsichord, the gilt sconce, a card-table, a set of tea china, the worked chairs, and screen . . . the ornamental china" and other furnishings.[1] Apparently she was dissatisfied, because in 1767 he wrote: "I suppose the blue room is too blue, the wood being the same color with the paper, and so looks too dark. I would have you . . . paint the wainscoat a dead white; paper the walls blue, and tack the gilt border round just above the surbase and under the cornice. . . . When this is done, I think it will look very well."[2]

Franklin's efforts in London proved fruitless and he returned to Philadelphia in 1775 to enjoy his new home. He soon took a seat in the Continental Congress and in 1777 was a member of a mission to Montreal to urge the Canadians to unite with the colonies. This futile trip was made by horseback, wagon and ship and was so exhausting that the seventy-one-year-old statesman thought he had not long to live.

But within a few months Franklin was being welcomed to France with overwhelming acclaim. After nine years of inestimable help to his country there, he came home to contribute to the Constitutional Convention.

Benjamin Franklin's library chair (Fig. 101) and Thomas Jefferson's windsor (Fig. 45) are exhibited in the American Philosophical Society Building on Independence Square in Philadelphia. It was in 1743 that Franklin proposed this organization of "ingenious Men residing in the several Colonies," and later he helped finance their building. As far back as 1798 a member wrote that their president sat in the "shabby arm chair which Franklin had long used as a desk chair and which he, himself, had occupied as president of the Society."[3] It is still upholstered in the same shabby brown leather.

Franklin, always resourceful, had had it constructed so that the seat could turn up to form a stepladder and he could reach the books on his highest shelves (Fig. 102). He had a similar chair, without the steps, that since 1822 has been the president's chair at Columbia University.

This kind of upholstered chair is often called an open armchair because of the open space between the arm and the seat. Chippendale and his contemporaries called them French chairs, which is very confusing because in America they seldom had either French rococo motifs or the French scroll foot. A set of elaborate open armchairs were made by Thomas Affleck, of Philadelphia, for Governor John Penn, grandson of the Proprietor (Fig. 103).

For upholstery on any of his chairs Chippendale frequently selected "the same kind of stuff as the Window Curtains."[4] He also used needlework, leather and haircloth. The latter came in several colors. He thought red morocco on his ribbon-back chairs would give "a fine Effect."[5]

The textiles at the Winterthur Museum form a vast collection in themselves. There one can see such seventeenth- and eighteenth-century fabrics as French satin lampas, Italian cut velvet, English Spitalfields brocade and American glazed wool. Among the innumerable colors are cherry-red moreen, blue silk damask, sea-green brocatelle, indigo resist-dyed linen and yellow homespun. Needlework such as petit point, the flame stitch, quillwork and crewelwork are also in evidence. The crewelwork hangings on one bed belonged to William Penn, those on another bed belonged to Thomas Hancock and later to his nephew John.

The superbly carved woodwork in one of the parlors at Winterthur came from a house in Philadelphia. The salmon-colored curtains at the windows are of French silk trimmed with matching needlepoint. Similar silk upholsters the furniture, an unprecedented assemblage of Philadelphia Chippendale—eight pieces with the very rare paw foot.

[1] Watson, *Annals of Philadelphia*, I, 206-7.
[2] *The Works of Benjamin Franklin*, ed. Jared Sparks, VII, 347.
[3] *Moreau de St. Mery's American Journey, 1793-1798*, ed. Kenneth and Anna Roberts, pp. 351-2.
[4] Chippendale, *The Gentleman and Cabinet-Maker's Director*, 3rd ed., Pl. IX-XIV.
[5] *Ibid.*, Pl. XV.

Fig. 101 CHIPPENDALE OPEN ARMCHAIR
presumed to have belonged to
Benjamin Franklin (1706-1790)
(American Philosophical Society, Philadelphia)

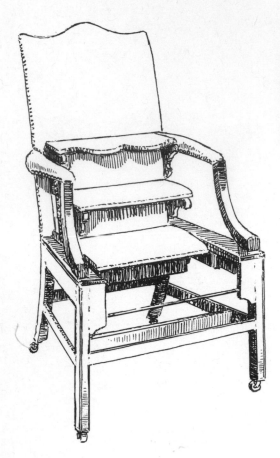

Fig. 102
Franklin's library chair with the seat raised (Fig. 102). Steps under the seat gave him access to books on the highest shelves. Upholstered chairs are called open armchairs when there is a space between the arm and seat.

Fig. 103
OPEN ARMCHAIR, one of a set believed to have been made, around 1765, for *Governor John Penn,* grandson of William Penn (Colonial Williamsburg, Williamsburg, Virginia). It has a bracket between the leg and seat rail, bellflowers and strapwork carved in the panel of the leg, and the block foot.

Fig. 104
CHIPPENDALE armchair with a shell at
the center of the top rail and tassels and
cord on each side, fluted stiles and Philadelphia arms (The Metropolitan Museum
of Art, New York City).

131

Fig. 105 CHIPPENDALE EASY CHAIR
presumed to have belonged to
Mary Ball Washington (*c.* 1708-1789)
(Mount Vernon, Virginia)

25. *CHIPPENDALE* (*c.* 1755-*c.* 1790)

Mahogany

> *Charles Allen . . . Lately from London and Paris, &c. Is removed to a shop of Mr. George Dowig's, at the sign of the Crown and Jewels, in Front Street . . . He makes all sorts of field, festoon, and canopy beds drapery, window curtains, stuffs sofas, settees, couches, French elbow, easy, corner, and back-stool chairs, . . . He puts up all sorts of paper hangings, and makes Venetian blinds for windows.*
>
> Pennsylvania Packet
> (Philadelphia) September 5, 1774

MARY, the youngest child of Joseph and Mary Ball, had scarcely reached her teens when she was orphaned in 1721. Her mother had asked Captain George Eskridge, an attorney and family friend, to be Mary's guardian. She left Mary a "good young Paceing horse together with a good silk plush side saddle," another horse, property, clothing, jewelry and household furnishings, including table linen "marked MB with inck."

In 1730 Mary became the second wife of Augustine Washington whose estate on the Potomac later became known as Wakefield.* Both their grandfathers, Colonel William Ball and John Washington, had come from England in the 1650's and had settled in the same part of Virginia. When the young Washingtons' first son was born, in 1732, they named him George, probably for Captain Eskridge.

In about 1740 the family moved to Ferry Farm on the Rappahannock, where Mr. Washington died in 1743. He willed several hundred acres to George and to each of his three younger sons and made provision for Betty, his only daughter. To Lawrence, a son by his first marriage, he left a plantation on the Potomac that Lawrence named Mount Vernon for the British Admiral Vernon under whom he had served.

In 1747 Lawrence secured a midshipman's warrant for George who also wanted naval training. Mary Ball Washington was a very able mother, but a determined one, and she refused to let her eldest go to sea, little knowing that she was thus altering the course of history.

In her late years Mrs. Washington was to move once again, this time to nearby Fredericksburg.* There the General paid her his last visit, just before departing for New York to become the first President of the United States.

A Chippendale easy chair that once belonged to Mary Ball Washington is now at Mount Vernon (Fig. 105). It is unusual because all four legs are cabriole. Stretchers were not commonly seen on Chippendale chairs with cabriole legs, except in New England (Fig. 106), but they were customary with the straight or Marlborough leg.

The Chippendale back stool, or upholstered chair without arms, was not a new type of chair. They were called "Bacstowylls" in an English inventory of 1436[1] and "backe stoules" in a British upholsterer's bill of 1611.[2] Perhaps the early back stools, like some of those in the Chippendale style, really were stools with all four legs alike. The backs of Chippendale back stools were not as high as the Queen Anne (Fig. 64). Robert Manwaring designed some with curved backs that influenced American chairmakers (Fig. 107).

The frames for easy chairs, back stools, sofas and other upholstered pieces were made by cabinetmakers and they were completed by upholsterers, originally called upholders. This was before the time of steel springs, so quantities of linen stuffing, horsehair or feathers were needed under the so-called "canvas" covering that was beneath the richer fabric.

Upholsterers, like carvers, sometimes had their own shops; at other times they were employed by cabinetmakers. They were the interior decorators of their day and supplied Venetian blinds, wallpaper and other needs, besides upholstering furniture and making curtains. They also made mattresses, and John Mason of Philadelphia advertised in 1770 that sleeping on his "Mattress-Beds" would "strengthen and brace up the nerves, . . . at this time of crisis, when our Liberty is tottering."[3] They continued, too, to make slip covers called "covers" or "cases." In 1751 Thomas Elfe of Charleston, South Carolina, advertised "tight and loose cases" for upholstered chairs,[4] and in 1762 Rebecca Weyman of the same city was making "easy chair cases for washing."[5]

Chippendale styled himself an upholsterer as well as a cabinetmaker in the third edition of the *Director*. His accounts tell us that he decorated the new house of David Garrick, the actor, in 1772. Green silk damask curtains were in the drawing room and the same damask covered the sofas and armchairs. For these Chippendale also supplied slip covers of green serge. He often chose serge, in the predominating color of the room, for slip covers, but he also used striped or checked linen or cotton.

[1] Downs, *American Furniture*, No. 98.
[2] "Cranborne Manor House," *Country Life*, June 14, 1924.
[3] Prime, *Arts and Crafts*, I, 209.
[4] *Ibid.*, I, 166.
[5] *Ibid.*, I, 217.

Fig. 106
CHIPPENDALE EASY chair with turned
stretchers which are as a rule found only
on New England easy chairs of this style
(David Stockwell, Wilmington, Delaware). The seat is curved in front and
has a loose cushion.

135

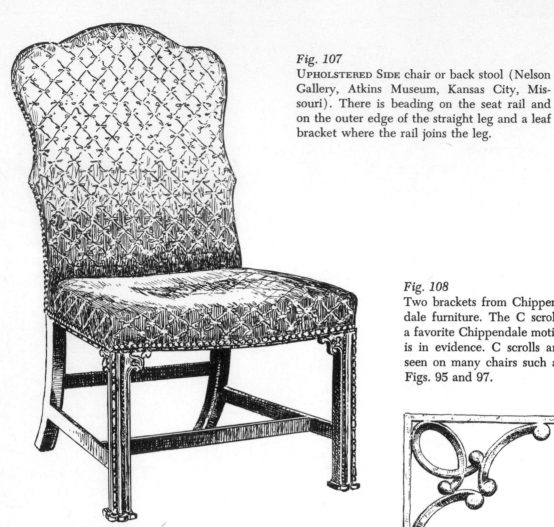

Fig. 107
UPHOLSTERED SIDE chair or back stool (Nelson Gallery, Atkins Museum, Kansas City, Missouri). There is beading on the seat rail and on the outer edge of the straight leg and a leaf bracket where the rail joins the leg.

Fig. 108
Two brackets from Chippendale furniture. The C scroll, a favorite Chippendale motif, is in evidence. C scrolls are seen on many chairs such as Figs. 95 and 97.

Fig. 109
A CHIPPENDALE chair back with four Gothic quatrefoils amidst the four banisters of the pierced splat (Mabel Brady Garvan Collection, Yale University Art Gallery, New Haven, Connecticut). There is leaf carving on the top rail and the stiles are fluted.

136

CHAPTER FIVE

Chairs of the Late Eighteenth Century

THE CLASSIC PERIOD

Hepplewhite
Sheraton

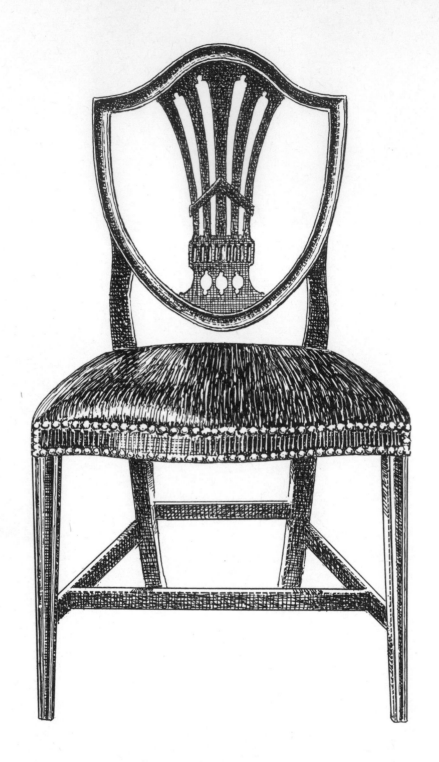

Fig. 110 HEPPLEWHITE CHAIR
presumed to have belonged to
John Hancock (1737-1793)
(Marblehead Historical Society, Lee Mansion,
Marblehead, Massachusetts)

26. *HEPPLEWHITE* (*c.* 1785-*c.* 1800)

Mahogany

> *Furniture—The Property of Benedict Arnold . . . will be sold by Public Vendue, under the Meal Market, Sundry Household and Kitchen Furniture, . . . Mahogany Dining and other Tables, Cases of Drawers, China and other Ware, Mahogany and Windsor Chairs . . . wearing Apparel, a small Library of Books . . . Late the property of Benedict Arnold, forfeited and sold according to law.*
>
> *Pennsylvania Packet*
> (Philadelphia) November 21, 1780

IN 1767 Governor Francis Bernard called Samuel Adams and his fellow patriots a "set of desperadoes" and complained that they were poisoning the minds of the people of Boston. When John Hancock, the richest young man in town, later joined the "desperadoes," he brought them considerable prestige. Hancock had lost his father, a minister, when he was a small boy and had been adopted by his uncle, Thomas Hancock, one of Boston's leading merchants. He was graduated from Harvard in 1754 and ten years later inherited his uncle's business and most of his fortune.

In time Hancock became particularly interested in Massachusetts politics and served nine terms as governor. He was elected a delegate to the Second Continental Congress and was made its president. Later he was greatly disappointed not to be chosen commander-in-chief of the army instead of George Washington, even though he had had no military experience. As president of Congress he was the first to sign the Declaration of Independence. With ample blank space before him he boldly and defiantly wrote his "John Hancock."

Several auctions of Hancock's abundant supply of household goods were held between 1793 and 1863. The advertisement for one of them, on the wharf at Boston, caught the eye of Captain Ephraim Chambers in April, 1795. He had sold the schoonerload of fish he had brought from Marblehead and while he was waiting for the tide to turn, he and his crew attended the sale in the Hancock house on Beacon Hill. "Just to start something," the Captain made a bid on six mahogany chairs. No bid followed and he and his men carried the chairs to the schooner and to Marblehead where they are proudly exhibited today.[1]

The Hancock chairs are in the classic style of Hepplewhite (Fig. 110), a far cry from the rococo style of Chippendale. To understand this decided change in furniture design we have to look back a few years.

Until the Revolution the wealthier colonists had been intent upon following the fashions of their English cousins. In 1771 William Eddis, a visitor from Britain, found "the quick importations of fashions . . . really astonishing." He was "almost inclined to believe" that a new fashion was "adopted earlier by the polished and affluent American, than by many persons in the great metropolis" (London). Eddis had less to say about the colonists' houses, but he found "many pleasant villas" and their interiors were "well fitted up and perfectly convenient." Styles in clothing and also in furniture presumably lagged much more in rural England and rural America than in the cities of either country.

After the first shots were fired at Lexington and Concord (where General Gage hoped to capture John Hancock and Samuel Adams), most Americans lost interest in the new modes of London. The cabinetmakers who were not drawn into the conflict continued to make furniture in the Chippendale style, while in England even Chippendale himself was making a part of his furniture in the Adam style.

The four Adam brothers, all architects, had traveled through Italy studying early Roman architecture and also the excavations of ancient cities. After their return to England Robert Adam, the leader, was made architect to the King. Soon the brothers were planning English houses in the classic style.

The decided change in architecture demanded a change in interior decoration. The Brothers Adam designed the wall decorations, textiles, furniture and accessories so that all would be harmonious. Their furniture designs (published only in their drawings of interiors) were made up for their clients by Thomas Chippendale, George Hepplewhite and other London cabinetmakers.

By the close of the Revolution the Adam style was no longer the height of fashion in England, and Americans turned to the newer Hepplewhite. The Hancock chairs are characteristic of the refined, formal Hepplewhite, a contrast to the heavy, robust Chippendale.

The Chippendale-Hepplewhite transition chair proved a desirable link between two such dissimilar styles (Fig. 111). It resembled the Chippendale style, but was lighter in scale, had the Hepplewhite serpentine top rail and often the Hepplewhite tapering legs. State senators in Maryland used such chairs until 1879 (Fig. 112). Meanwhile, shield-back Hepplewhite chairs (Fig. 113) were being occupied by Connecticut senators.

[1] Mabel M. Swan, "Furniture of His Excellency John Hancock," *Antiques,* March, 1937.

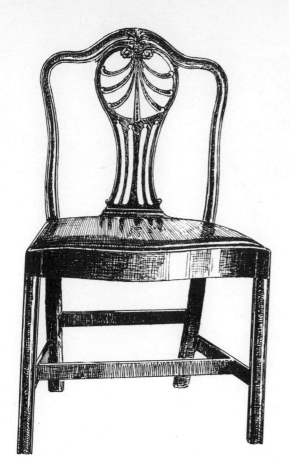

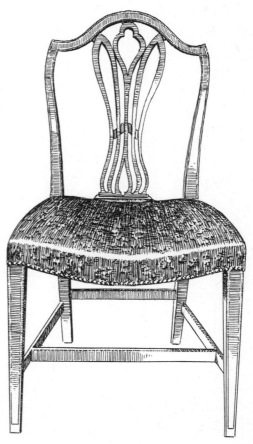

Fig. 111
CHIPPENDALE-HEPPLEWHITE transition chair, like a Chippendale chair except for the serpentine top rail of a Hepplewhite shield-back ·(Nutting's *Furniture Treasury*). The inverted anthemion or honeysuckle design in the top of the splat is of classic origin.

Fig. 112
CHIPPENDALE-HEPPLEWHITE transition chair, formerly in the Maryland senate chamber (Maryland Historical Society, Baltimore). Lighter in scale than a Chippendale chair, it has the straight tapering leg of the Hepplewhite style and a concave seat.

141

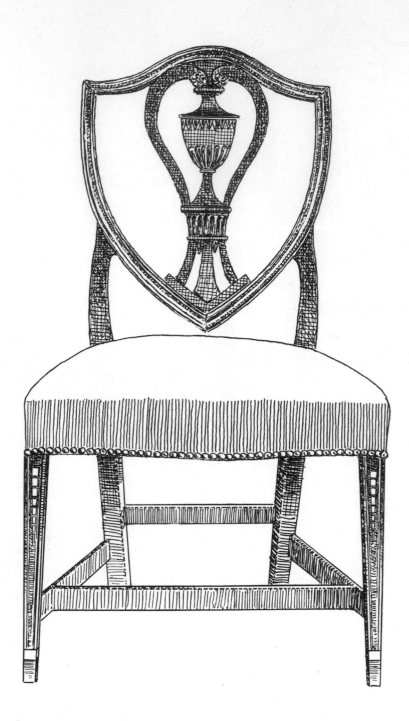

Fig. 113
This HEPPLEWHITE chair, formerly used
by the Connecticut state senators, has a
shield-shaped back with an urn in the
splat and pendant inlay on the tapering
legs (Connecticut State Library, Hartford).

27. *HEPPLEWHITE* (*c.* 1785-*c.* 1800)

Mahogany

The Gentlemen Cabinet and Chair Makers are requested to meet in Church alley tomorrow Morning, the 4th of July, at 8 o'clock, to proceed from thence to join the Federal Procession. Every Master will inform his Journeymen that their company is expected. Likewise furnish their Apprentices with the Badges agreed on for the day. Jonathan Gostelowe, Chairman.

Pennsylvania Packet
(Philadelphia) July 3, 1788

CHARLES CARROLL, like his father and grandfather before him, went to France for his schooling. He was only ten when he sailed from Maryland and twenty-eight when he returned in 1765. He had spent the last few years in Paris and London. His father deeded Carrollton to him and he added "of Carrollton" to his signature to distinguish himself from his father and cousins, all named Charles Carroll.

His Irish-born grandfather emigrated to Maryland in 1668 after he was appointed attorney-general of the Colony. British laws soon denied him the privilege of holding office because he was a Roman Catholic. For the same reason Charles Carroll expected to have no part in politics, but before long he and William Paca, Samuel Chase and others were involved in Maryland's pre-Revolutionary agitation. In 1776 he accompanied Benjamin Franklin to Canada. His religion and his facility with French made him particularly suited for the mission (p. 127).

As a member of the Continental Congress and its Board of War, he spent three months at Valley Forge in 1778 assisting General Washington with the army's reorganization. One of his later public offices was that of Senator in the first Senate of the United States, where he was influential in setting the precedents of Senatorial tradition.

Charles Carroll of Carrollton owned some seventy thousand acres. He was also interested in such projects as the Baltimore and Ohio Railroad and participated in its opening ceremonies in 1828. He was the only surviving signer of the Declaration of Independence, after the deaths of John Adams and Thomas Jefferson, on July 4, 1826, its fiftieth anniversary. Scholarly always, at ninety-three Carroll was still reading the classics with a preference for "the philosophic works of Cicero."

Three shield-back chairs from Carrollton are enriched by plumes, drapery, pendant bellflowers, rosettes and other carved motifs (Fig. 114). Shield-back and oval-back chairs had been introduced by the Brothers Adam and were made still more fashionable by George Hepplewhite. The base of the shield was either pointed or curved and frequently a fan or a part of a rosette was carved or inlaid there (Fig. 115).

Hepplewhite's *The Cabinet-Maker and Upholsterer's Guide* was published in 1788, two years after his death. His widow, Alice, is assumed to be the "A" of A. Hepplewhite and Company which brought out three editions, the last in 1794. She also maintained his shop in Redcross Street, Cripplegate, London. Mrs. Hepplewhite seems to have had more ambition than education, since she once signed a legal paper "Aleas," later corrected to Alice.

"Chairs in general are made of mahogany," said the *Guide* and in the United States this was more true than in England. The book told of "a new and very elegant fashion" there of finishing chairs made of other woods "with paint or japanned work" in colors suitable to the room. They were decorated with painted motifs. This innovation apparently was not immediately taken up here, but in 1796 twenty-four painted oval-back chairs (Fig. 124) were ordered from Philadelphia by Elias Hasket Derby of Salem, Massachusetts (p. 171).[1]

When made of mahogany, the wood in the shield and its supports was often molded and had a beading on each edge (Fig. 116). The exact dimensions were given in Hepplewhite's *Guide*, but it was noted that they could be "adapted to the size of the room or the pleasure of the purchaser."

The straight leg that tapers toward the floor is considered a mark of the classic style, even though Chippendale also designed a few chairs with a tapering leg. Hepplewhite chair legs were much smaller than the Chippendale straight legs and they always tapered. They were plain (Fig. 122), molded (Fig. 110) or fluted (Fig. 116), and made with or without a spade foot. Often a band of inlay was used in lieu of a foot (Figs. 113, 115). Stretchers were a matter of choice. Eighteenth-century cabinetmakers were taught to place stretchers so that they

Fig. 114 Hepplewhite Chair
presumed to have belonged to
Charles Carroll of Carrollton (1737-1832)
(The Henry Francis du Pont Winterthur Museum,
Winterthur, Delaware)

Fig. 115
HEPPLEWHITE chair said to have been
owned by *Alexander Hamilton* (1757-
1804), (Charles K. Davis, Fairfield, Connecticut). It is unusual in that the top of
the shield is straight, and it is profusely
inlaid with pendant bellflowers and other
motifs.

would be flush with the outside of the leg (Fig. 114).

Cabinetmakers began their training at an early age. In 1795 one of them
advertised in the Norfolk, Virginia, *Herald* for apprentices "from 11 to 14 years."[2]
That same year *The Journeyman Cabinet and Chair-Maker Philadelphia Book
of Prices* stated that "Day Men" were "to work from six to six o'clock, the Em-
ployer to find Candles."[3]

[1] Mabel M. Swan, "Where Elias Hasket Derby Bought His Furniture," *Antiques,* November, 1931.
[2] Prime, *Arts and Crafts,* II, 169.
[3] Harrold E. Gillingham, "A Philadelphia Cabinetmaker and His Price List," *Antiques,* September, 1930, p. 250.

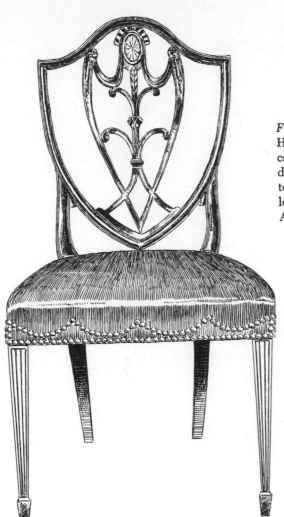

Fig. 116
HEPPLEWHITE chair with five feathers carved within the splat, with patera and drapery above them; nail heads are festooned across the seat rail and the fluted leg has a spade foot (Nelson Gallery, Atkins Museum, Kansas City, Missouri).

Fig. 117
A Hepplewhite design for a tea tray, with patera at the center. The motifs include the urn, foliage, bellflower and bowknot (Pl. 59, *The Cabinet-Maker and Upholsterer's Guide*, 3rd ed.).

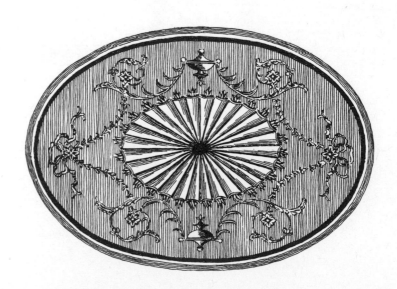

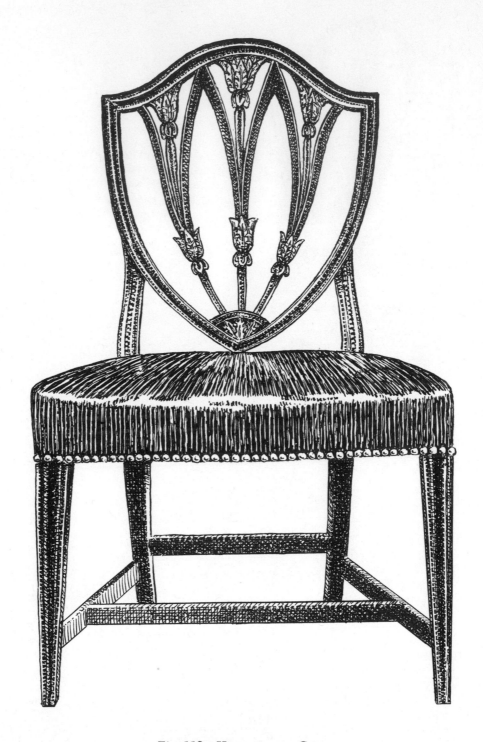

Fig. 118   Hepplewhite Chair
presumed to have belonged to
Thomas Jefferson (1743-1826)
(Thomas Jefferson Memorial Foundation, Monticello, Virginia)

28. *HEPPLEWHITE* (*c.* 1785-*c.* 1800)

Mahogany

> *Samuel Walton, Cabinet and Chair-Maker, At his Warehouse, No. 17, in Spruce-street . . . Philadelphia, Makes and sells all kinds of Household Furniture, of the newest and most elegant patterns, which have been lately imported from Europe . . . Orders from gentlemen in any of the United States, or West-India Islands, will be gratefully acknowledged, punctually attended to, and forwarded with the utmost expedition.*
>
> *Pennsylvania Mercury*
> (Philadelphia) September 9, 1785

WHILE living in France Thomas Jefferson became imbued with the classic style of architecture. From there he sent plans for the new capitol of Virginia at Richmond, the first public building in the nation to be patterned after the Greek temple. Jefferson was an architect by avocation and designed several Virginia houses besides carefully drafting the plans for his beloved Monticello. In his declining years he was the architect for the new University of Virginia at nearby Charlottesville, and those who have viewed its rotunda, pavilions and serpentine brick walls have an added appreciation for his many accomplishments.

Jefferson made innumerable contributions to the culture of his countrymen. As a connoisseur of art he formed valuable collections of statuary and portraits, particularly of his European and American contemporaries. He had a lifelong love for music and for books, and his library became the nucleus for the Library of Congress. Besides the many facets of his superior mind, he had a sincere devotion to his fellow man. An English admirer once wrote, "His heart was warmed with a love for the whole human race; a bonhomie which fixed your attention the instant he spoke."

After Jefferson retired from public life Monticello had an endless stream of visitors, many of them uninvited. This was an added financial burden to the aging statesman who was then far from affluent. A critical Bostonian who came to Monticello in 1814 commented on "the state of the chairs" in the dining room: "They had leather bottoms stuffed with hair, but the bottoms were completely worn through and the hair sticking out in all directions."[1]

The throngs who visit Monticello today see some of the chairs that so disturbed the Bostonian. They are in the Hepplewhite style and have been reupholstered in leather (Fig. 118). Thomas Jefferson, George Washington and others who owned large plantations had their own cabinetmakers. Sketches of furniture have been found among Jefferson's papers, with explicit directions to his craftsmen. The less skillful workmanship on a few of the dining room chairs leads authorities to believe that they may have been copies made at Monticello.[2]

The shield backs have curved banisters and floral motifs much like a design in Hepplewhite's book. American cabinetmakers followed some of the patterns closely (Fig. 119), but they also made many adaptations just as they had of Chippendale's designs. Perhaps it was the intention of the authors merely to "guide" or "direct" as the titles of their books imply.

Hepplewhite emphasized the use of inlay, but he also liked carving. Satinwood and other light-colored woods inlaid against the dark mahogany were very effective and brought out the delicacy of detail. Baltimore and Annapolis craftsmen made outstanding examples.

The motifs reflect the classic influence quite as much as the chairs themselves. The classic urn or vase was often seen at the center of a pierced splat (Fig. 120). The shape of the urn on the chairs made in Hartford for the Connecticut Senate (Fig. 113) differs considerably from the urn on chairs made in Rhode Island and Massachusetts (Fig. 121).

Drapery festoons or swags were much in evidence (Fig. 120). They were of classic origin, as were the rosette and the Greek anthemion or honeysuckle. The latter was often found on the Chippendale-Hepplewhite transition chairs (Fig. 111). The patera took its name from the circular or oval patera or platelike dish used by the Romans (Fig. 117).

Bellflowers, also called husks, were an ancient motif. They are carved in pendant form on the Charles Carroll chair (Fig. 114) and are inlaid profusely on chairs that belonged to Alexander Hamilton (Fig. 115). His chairs are unusual because the top of the shield is straight.

Wheat heads, known as wheat ears in England, were a favorite Hepplewhite

Fig. 119
A Hepplewhite pattern closely followed by American chairmakers: Three-feather design within a splat surmounted by foliage (Pl. 6, *The Cabinet-Maker and Upholsterer's Guide*, 3rd ed.).

motif (Fig. 120), but feathers or plumes were a greater favorite. It is possible that Hepplewhite first used them on a chair mentioned in the *Guide* that had been "executed with good effect for his Royal Highness the Prince of Wales." The three-feather device, the heraldic emblem of the Prince, no doubt was used to entice royal favor, but three feathers and four or five feathers (Fig. 124) also became popular in the new republic.

[1] Kimball, *The Furnishings of Monticello,* p. 23.
[2] *Ibid.*, p. 23.

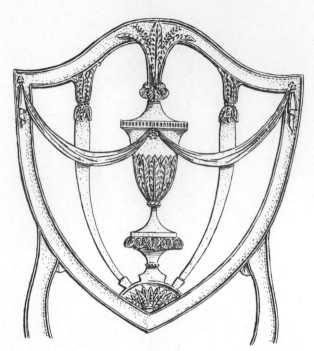

Fig. 120

HEPPLEWHITE chair with carving attributed to Samuel McIntyre of Salem, Massachusetts (Karolik Collection, Museum
of Fine Arts, Boston). The vase on a
pedestal has wheat heads above it, and
drapery is festooned across the vase and
the two curved bars. There is a pair of
similar chairs at the Art Institute of
Chicago.

Fig. 121

HEPPLEWHITE chair with a vase or urn
and festooned bands that are quite unlike those on Fig. 120; the fan is carved
at the base of the shield which is rounded
rather than pointed (Karolik Collection,
Museum of Fine Arts). This chair back
was favored in Rhode Island and Massachusetts; there is a pair of similar chairs
at the Rhode Island School of Design in
Providence.

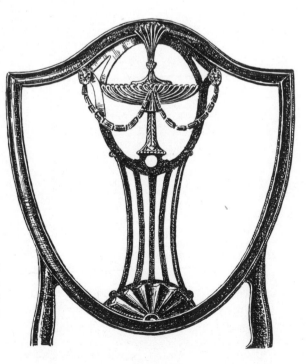

152

29. *HEPPLEWHITE* (*c.* 1785-*c.* 1800)

Mahogany

> *Looking Glasses, Come and see, An assortment of elegant Pier and Sconce Looking Glasses, Toilet and Dressing do. from one dollar to twenty . . . Beautiful Prints, Plain, striped and Figured Hair Seatings, . . . at No. 75, South Front Street, . . . John M'Elwee.*
> *Federal Gazette*
> (Philadelphia) November 4, 1794

JAMES MADISON was in Philadelphia as a member of Congress when he caught a glimpse of Dolley Payne Todd, a widow in her early twenties. Soon Dolley was dashing off a note to a friend: "Aaron Burr says that 'the great little Madison' has asked to see me this evening." Though she towered above his five feet, four inches and was nearly twenty years his junior, they became singularly devoted and were married in September, 1794, at the Virginia home of Dolley's sister and brother-in-law, a nephew and namesake of George Washington.

Madison had been an avid student while at Princeton and continued to be so throughout his life. He was drawn into public life in Virginia well before becoming a member of the Continental Congress at twenty-nine. By the time he took part in the Constitutional Convention, he was a recognized authority on government, and while he was there justly earned the name of "Father of the Constitution."

He was never a colorful statesman and was serious and withdrawn at public affairs. These traits were admirably offset by the charm and aplomb of Mrs. Madison. She dressed resplendently and had an especial fondness for plumed turbans, a great contrast to the attire of her Quaker girlhood. She was gifted at putting guests at their ease and her weekly "drawing rooms" at the White House attracted multitudes.

Fig. 122 HEPPLEWHITE HEART-BACK CHAIR
presumed to have belonged to
James Madison (1751-1836)
(Smithsonian Institution, Washington, D.C.)

In times of stress Dolley Madison also was equal to the occasion. When the British neared Washington in 1814, she calmly wrote her sister that she had saved Cabinet papers "but our private property must be sacrificed." A friend trying to hasten her departure was "in very bad humor . . . because I insist upon waiting until the large picture of General Washington is secured."

A Hepplewhite chair said to have been James Madison's is called a heart-back because the intersecting curves of the shield give it the appearance of a heart (Fig. 122). In 1795, just after the Madison wedding, Philadelphia chairmakers listed "Heart back" chairs in the *Book of Prices* and the account book of John Janvier, a young Delaware cabinetmaker, discloses that he made several the same year.[1] The Madison chair has been altered; the seat was raised and the legs were cut off, and later it was inexpertly restored and casters were attached.

Thomas Sheraton published his book so soon after Hepplewhite's *Guide* that there was much overlapping of styles. A shield-back similar to the one from Carrollton (Fig. 114) was in Sheraton's book, and Hepplewhite designed more rectangular backs than he did shield and oval ones combined. It is only for convenience and simplification that we now call all shield- and oval-back chairs Hepplewhite and all rectangular-back Sheraton.

Most of the oval-back chairs (Fig. 124) came from Philadelphia and Baltimore, but they were never in great demand in this country. Hepplewhite chairs were weak in construction because the shield or oval back had so little support. A few chairs with a modified shield back (Fig. 125) were made in Baltimore.

Seats of Hepplewhite chairs were narrower in back than in front and the side rails often were curved. The front seat rail at times was serpentine (Fig. 110), even though Philadelphia chairmakers charged more for "A serpentine or circular front" (Fig. 114) than for a straight front. Some seats were concave or hollowed (Fig. 112).

Hepplewhite suggested cane seats "with cushions," but Americans appear not to have been interested. Slip seats were seen less than those with upholstery covering the rails. The latter were often decorated with nails in festoons (Fig. 116) or straight lines (Fig. 110). Upholstery extends only halfway over the rails on the Carroll chair (Fig. 114), a practice followed mostly in Maryland.

The *Guide* recommended "horsehair, plain, striped, chequered &c" for upholstery, and red or blue morocco leather. Advertisements indicate the quantities of haircloth available, and a "Manufactory" near Baltimore was offering morocco in 1793.[2] Other fabrics also were used, often in stripes or small classic patterns.

155

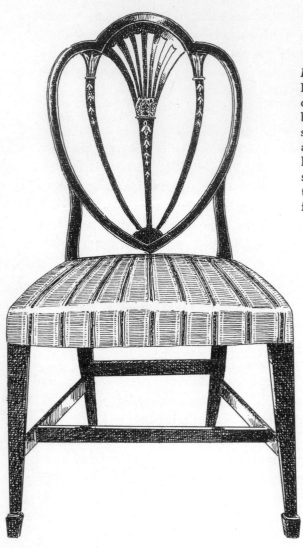

Fig. 123

HEPPLEWHITE HEART-BACK chair with delicate inlay on the back, said to have been owned by **Samuel Chase,** patriot, signer of the Declaration of Independence and justice of the Supreme Court (Maryland Historical Society, Baltimore). The stretchers are flush with the outside of the legs as they are on all 18th-century furniture.

The intense, vivid colors of the Queen Anne and Chippendale styles were giving way to more delicate hues, in keeping with the classic influence. As early as 1784 a paper hanger was advertising in Baltimore that he painted rooms "in an elegant manner, Verditure blue, Prussian blue, pea-green, straw, stone, slate, cream, cloth or pink colours."[3]

[1] Leon de Valinger, Jr., "John Janvier, Delaware Cabinetmaker," *Antiques,* January, 1942.
[2] Prime, *Arts and Crafts,* II, 203.
[3] *Ibid.,* I, 279.

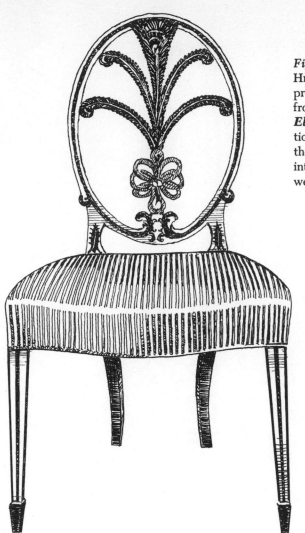

Fig. 124
HEPPLEWHITE PAINTED OVAL-BACK chair, probably one of the twenty-four ordered from Philadelphia in 1796 (p. 144) by *Elias Hasket Derby* (Karolik Collection, Museum of Fine Arts, Boston). Here there are five peacock feathers above the intricate bowknot. Some of Derby's chairs were decorated with ostrich plumes.

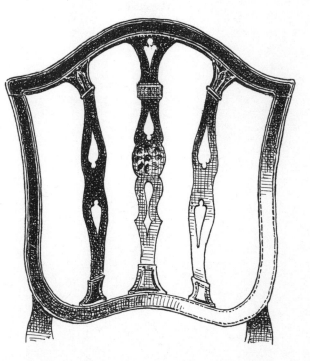

Fig. 125
HEPPLEWHITE chairs with this modified shield back, with a serpentine rail at the base, were made in Baltimore (*Antiques*, September, 1930). This chair is believed to have been the property of *Charles Carroll,* the barrister, of Annapolis and Baltimore.

Fig. 126 SHERATON CHAIR
presumed to have belonged to
Stephen Girard (1750-1831)
(Girard College, Philadelphia)

30. *SHERATON* (*c*. 1795-*c*. 1810)

Mahogany, unpainted

Other woods, painted

THE *Jeune Bébé* bound for New York from the West Indies in May, 1776, was beset by storms. Captain Stephen Girard's troubles mounted when a British frigate searched his sloop and seized his best mariner. With difficulty he brought the crippled *Jeune Bébé* to Philadelphia, the nearest port.

This was the captain's first sight of the city that was to be his home for the rest of his life. He had gone to sea from Bordeaux, France, his birthplace, at fourteen, but at twenty-six he had decided to become a merchant ship owner. He opened a small shop in Philadelphia and in the years that followed his business grew to incredible proportions. His several ships sailed to Europe and the West Indies, and in 1812 he established the Bank of Stephen Girard.

The next year the United States was desperately in need of funds to fight the war with Britain, but sold less than half of a sixteen-million-dollar bond issue. The Secretary of the Treasury appealed to John Jacob Astor and to Stephen Girard and they underwrote the balance.

Girard was never accepted socially in Philadelphia, even when he became a frequent host to Napoleon's brother Joseph Bonaparte, the exiled King of Spain. Scant appreciation had been given him for his enlightened service as manager of the hospital for yellow fever victims in 1793. He was considered a miser, but when his will was read his farseeing philanthropies became known. The residuary fund founded a school for fatherless boys from six to eighteen years of age. It increased from six million dollars in 1833 to approximately ninety million in 1956. By then over 16,000 boys had attended Girard College in Philadelphia.

In 1806 Ephraim Haines, a Philadelphia cabinetmaker, billed Girard for "12 chairs one sofa 2 pier tables and 4 stools."[1] They were in the Sheraton style (Fig. 126). Sheraton, like Hepplewhite, was influenced by the classic revival and many of his designs reveal his dependence upon French interpretation of the contemporary classicism. Some of his chairs are very similar to those of Louis XVI (Fig. 164).

The most distinctive feature of a Sheraton chair is the rectangular back with its cross bar just above the seat. This cross bar gave the chair a stability which was lacking in the Hepplewhite shield-back. Sheraton chairs have top rails that are straight (Fig. 126) or curved (Fig. 127). When the center of the top rail is raised, it is often a continuation of the narrow banisters (Fig. 128) usually found on each side of a central splat (Fig. 131). If there is no central splat, chair backs have a number of banisters in different sizes and shapes (Figs. 126, 127, 130).

Stephen Girard imported ebony for his Sheraton furniture, but mahogany was customary. It was often reeded, like much of the furniture of Louis XVI. Reeding was the counterpart to fluting, a series of ridges or reeds rather than a series of grooves or flutes. Sheraton thought it preferable to fluting "in point of strength" and nearly equal to it in appearance.[2]

Thomas Sheraton brought out *The Cabinet-Maker and Upholsterer's Drawing-Book* in parts, between 1791 and 1793. He gave instructions in "the art of making perspective drawings" so it was, in reality, a drawing book. He also wrote at length on geometry and the classic orders. In addition to his furniture patterns, he showed detailed drawings of motifs and moldings "to enrich and embellish" them (Fig. 133). He criticized his predecessors for omitting both the drawing instructions and the detailed designs. His aim was to make his book "permanently useful . . . and to unite with usefulness the taste of the times."[3]

A third edition of the *Drawing-Book* appeared in 1802 when he was publishing his *Dictionary*. Later he began his *Encyclopedia* which was never finished. By then furniture fashions were changing and his patterns lacked the refinement and simplicity of those in the *Drawing-Book*.

Sheraton considered Chippendale's *Director* "masterly in its designs" but

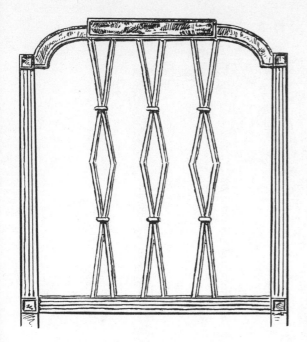

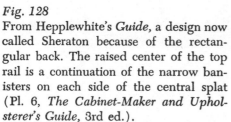

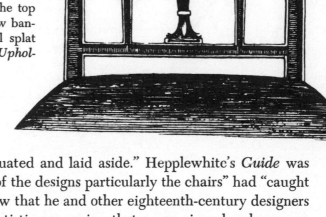

Fig. 127
Back of a SHERATON chair believed to
have been owned by *Elizabeth Derby
West,* daughter of Elias Hasket Derby
(Karolik Collection, Museum of Fine
Arts, Boston). The triple-lattice back is
entirely reeded except for the curved top
rail.

Fig. 128
From Hepplewhite's *Guide,* a design now
called Sheraton because of the rectangular back. The raised center of the top
rail is a continuation of the narrow banisters on each side of the central splat
(Pl. 6, *The Cabinet-Maker and Upholsterer's Guide,* 3rd ed.).

that it had been "wholly antiquated and laid aside." Hepplewhite's *Guide* was
"not without merit" but "some of the designs particularly the chairs" had "caught
the decline." Sheraton little knew that he and other eighteenth-century designers
had reached a high point of artistic expression that never since has been sur-
passed.

[1] Nancy McClelland, *Duncan Phyfe and the English Regency,* pp. 228-30.
[2] Hornor, *Bluebook,* p. 251.
[3] Thomas Sheraton, *The Cabinet-Maker and Upholsterer's Drawing-Book,* 3rd ed., p. 292.

Fig. 129
A Sheraton pattern that found favor in
America, called a racquet back from the
shape of the splat (Pl. 28, *The Cabinet-
Maker and Upholsterer's Drawing-Book,*
3rd ed.).

Fig. 130
SHERATON armchair, delicate but not
fragile, has reeded arm supports and legs,
and fan carving at the top of each reeded
banister (Minneapolis Institute of Arts).

163

Fig. 131 SHERATON CHAIR
presumed to have belonged to
George Washington (1732-1799)
and later to
Nelly Custis Lewis (1779-1852)
(Smithsonian Institution, Washington, D.C.)

31. *SHERATON* (*c*. 1795-*c*. 1810)

Mahogany, unpainted

Other woods, painted

"MISS CUSTIS was married abt. Candle light to Mr. Lawe. Lewis," George Washington noted in his diary on his birthday in 1799. No one had been more surprised than the General when Nelly Custis and Lawrence Lewis disclosed their wedding plans. Washington had not "the smallest suspicion that such an affair was in agitation." Nelly had several suitors, including the son of Charles Carroll of Carrollton, but he had never considered Lawrence, his nephew, one of them.

Nelly and her brother had been adopted by General and Mrs. Washington in 1781, shortly after the death of their father, John Parke Custis, Mrs. Washington's son. Lawrence Lewis had lived at Mount Vernon since 1797 because the General thought him a "fit and Proper" person to assist there, especially in entertaining the ever-present guests.

A few months after the wedding, Washington set aside two thousand acres for the young couple. His old friend Dr. William Thornton, architect for the United States Capitol, later drew plans for their manor house. The General thought Gray's Hill on the property "a most beautiful Site for a Gentleman's Seat," but he was never to see Woodlawn,* the stately late Georgian mansion built there.

From the portico of Woodlawn there is a breathtaking panoramic view of the Potomac. In the impressive hall with its winding stair, Nelly and Lawrence Lewis received the Marquis de Lafayette, Presidents of the United States and countless other friends. In the drawing room Nelly played the harpsichord and her husband the violin or flute, to the delight of their children. Everywhere at Woodlawn there is evidence of the gracious living that was a part of the tradition of the owners.

Mrs. Washington bequeathed to her granddaughter a number of the furnishings at Mount Vernon, among them "twelve chairs with Green Bottoms to be selected by herself." They were from a set of twenty-four chairs made for the banquet room in 1797 by John Aitkin of Philadelphia (Fig. 131).

Classic motifs from Sheraton's patterns are seen on the delicately carved back. They include the pierced urn at the center of the splat, the drapery and leaf carving. Sheraton also liked the fan motif, the rosette, bellflower, bowknot, wheat head and three feathers. The urn took different forms on Sheraton chairs (Fig. 132) just as it had on Hepplewhite patterns.

Sheraton's patterns in the *Drawing-Book* usually have the turned tapering leg, but American chairmakers were more inclined to use the square tapering leg, sometimes inlaid. When they chose the turned leg, it was plain, reeded (Fig. 134), or carved and reeded (Fig. 126), and there were some differences in the turned foot.

Something of Thomas Sheraton's personality, ability and way of life is given us in the *Memoirs* of Adam Black, a Scottish publisher. Black arrived in London in 1804, a youth in need of employment. He found work with Sheraton but stayed only a week, ashamed to take the "miserable" pay "from the poor man."

Sheraton lived in "an obscure street, his house half shop, half dwelling house." Adam Black found "dirt and bugs"—no compliment to Mrs. Sheraton's housekeeping. He had tea with them one day and learned that they possessed only two china cups. Mrs. Sheraton and their daughter used small porringers.

Thomas Sheraton wore a threadbare black coat and looked like a worn-out preacher. Black confided to his diary, "He [Sheraton] is a man of many talents . . . understands the cabinet business . . . he has been . . . a preacher; he is a scholar, writes well; draws, in my opinion, masterly; is an author, bookseller, stationer and teacher."

In the third edition of the *Drawing-Book* Sheraton complained that his "vast expense" had deprived him "of the emolument that might have been expected from so large a subscription."[1] It is surprising that he obtained seven hundred

Fig. 132
SHERATON chair spoken of as an urn-and-scroll-back because of the pattern of the splat (The Metropolitan Museum of Art, New York City). This turned and reeded leg does not have leaf carving like that of the Girard chair (Fig. 126). A square and tapered leg with line inlay is seen on the Washington-Custis chair (Fig. 131).

Fig. 133
A detail from one of Sheraton's designs.
It appears at the top of a carved and
reeded leg (No. 43, Pl. 2, *The Cabinet-
Maker and Upholsterer's Drawing-Book*).

subscribers (five hundred were cabinetmakers), but few were "persons of distinction" who had been helpful to Chippendale.

Sheraton was born in Stockton-on-Tees in 1750 and died in Broad Street,
Soho, London, in 1806. The *Gentleman's Magazine* for November, 1806, mentioned him in its section "Obituary, with Anecdotes, of remarkable Persons":
Sheraton was "a very honest, well-disposed man of an acute and enterprising
disposition," yet they feared he had left his family in "distressed circumstances."

[1] Sheraton, *The Cabinet-Maker and Upholsterer's Drawing-Book,* 3rd ed., p. 23.

Fig. 134
SHERATON OPEN ARMCHAIR, called a
Martha Washington chair (Nutting's
Furniture Treasury). The scroll under
the arm where it meets the arm post, and
the inlaid panel on the block below the
arm post, are both unusually good features. The turned front legs are fitted
with brass cups attached to casters.

Fig. 135 Sheraton Armchair
presumed to have belonged to
Elias Hasket Derby (1739-1799)
(Karolik Collection, Museum of Fine Arts, Boston)

32. *SHERATON* (*c.* 1795-*c.* 1810)

Mahogany, unpainted

Other woods, painted

Richard Wevill, Upholsterer . . . opposite Congress Hall, in Chestnut Street . . . Bed and Window Cornices manufactured in the newest taste, gilt or painted, to suit the furniture . . .
Just imported in the Active, *from London . . . a quantity of Hair Seating, Gold Leaf, . . . fine Sattin-wood, tulip wood, and purple wood Veneers, and an assortment of Stringing [line inlay] &c. for Cabinet-makers.*

Federal Gazette
(Philadelphia) November 16, 1799

"IN the genteel society of Boston I could perceive no distinction from my own country," wrote John Bernard, an English actor who came to America in 1797. He found that they "wore the same clothes, spoke the same language . . . and in their houses the last modes of London were observable in nearly every article of ornament or utility." Charles Bulfinch was planning the houses for the "genteel" Bostonians while Samuel McIntyre and other able architects were at work elsewhere in New England.

The most magnificent mansion built by Samuel McIntyre of Salem was torn down long ago. It was completed in 1799 for Elias Hasket Derby, the foremost of the shipping merchants whose daring and competence brought so much wealth to New England and to themselves. He was content to live in a modest dwelling,* but his wife persuaded him to spend lavishly on his pretentious McIntyre house and its furnishings.

Derby ships, bravely flying the unfamiliar flag of the United States, entered ports throughout the world. They returned with exotic cargoes from Batavia, Canton and Bombay. At the Derby Wharf* in Salem the greater part was reloaded onto smaller vessels sailing to America's coastal cities.

These coastwise cargoes often carried New England furniture. Cabinet-makers also put their handiwork aboard ships destined for far places such as South America and the East Indies. At least twice Derby's captains arranged to sell Salem cabinetwork at auction in Calcutta. A delicately inlaid secretary-bookcase in the Winterthur Museum bears the label of Nehemiah Adams of Salem. It was found, in recent years, in Capetown, South Africa.[1]

A part of Mr. Derby's furniture, in the Boston Museum of Fine Arts, was the gift of his great-granddaughter, the late Martha C. Karolik (nee Codman).[2] The carving on some of it is attributed to Samuel McIntyre, a noteworthy carver and cabinetmaker as well as architect (Fig. 120). A pair of upholstered arm-chairs are believed to be the work of John Seymour of Boston (Fig. 135).

They have the Sheraton turned and reeded arm support and leg seen on many of the higher-backed Martha Washington chairs (Fig. 134). The latter were the open armchairs of the Hepplewhite and Sheraton styles, much lighter in scale than the Chippendale (Figs. 101, 103). Those with the concave arm support and square tapered leg might be called either Hepplewhite or Sheraton (Fig. 136). They have been termed Martha Washington chairs since early in the nineteenth century,[3] but there is no evidence that Mrs. Washington possessed one.

Both Sheraton and Hepplewhite designed chaise longues and Hepplewhite also designed one easy chair. It has such large and cumbersome wings that it appears top heavy (Fig. 137). Our craftsmen made adaptations of it (Fig. 176). During the century, from the Queen Anne style through the Sheraton, there also were sofas with upholstered backs and settees with two or more chair backs.

Painted Sheraton chairs, although not widely used in America, have been found in green, gray, red, black, white and other colors. They are decorated with striping, classic motifs and scenes in colors or in gold leaf (Fig. 138). Sheraton liked "white and gold" or "japan painting interspersed with a little gilding . . . for a lively effect." He called them fancy chairs, but they were partly of joined construction and if they are spoken of as painted Sheraton they can be distinguished from the innumerable fancy chairs, largely of stick construction, that also were painted or japanned (p. 192). Curved seats that appear on several of Sheraton's patterns were seldom adopted here except on fancy chairs (Fig. 147).

For his drawing room chairs, and supposedly for others, Sheraton favored French printed silk or the chintz that could "be had of various patterns on purpose for chair seats, together with borders to suit them." He also mentioned "the

Fig. 136

MARTHA WASHINGTON chair with concave arm supports and the square, tapering leg of Hepplewhite-Sheraton styles (Mabel Brady Garvan Collection, Yale University Art Gallery, New Haven, Connecticut). Martha Washington chairs were lighter in scale than Chippendale open armchairs; both should have the curved top rail.

Easy Chair

Fig. 137
EASY chair from Hepplewhite's *Guide.*
The wings are so large and cumbersome
that the chair appears top-heavy (Pl. 15,
Cabinet-Maker and Upholsterer's Guide,
3rd ed.). See Fig. 176 for an American
Hepplewhite easy chair with smaller
wings which came from Mount Vernon.

sprigged figure" and several chairs in the *Drawing-Book* have upholstery in
narrow stripes or have a large medallion at the center.

A medallion decorates a blue-green and gold haircloth seat of a chair owned
by a descendant of the maker, John George, who manufactured haircloth in
Philadelphia shortly after the Revolution.[4] The original haircloth, still on the
chairs from Mount Vernon and Woodlawn, has a large medallion and a "sprigged
figure" (Fig. 131). Now faded, it once was green on a yellow background.[5]

[1] Mabel M. Swan, "Coastwise Cargoes of Venture Furniture," *Antiques,* April, 1949.
[2] Edwin J. Hipkiss, *Eighteenth-Century American Arts, The M. and M. Karolik Collection.*
[3] Mabel M. Swan, "Newburyport Furnituremakers," *Antiques,* April, 1945.
[4] *Antiques,* July, 1949, p. 57.
[5] Marion S. Carson, "Washington Furniture at Mount Vernon," *The American Collector,* May,
1947.

174

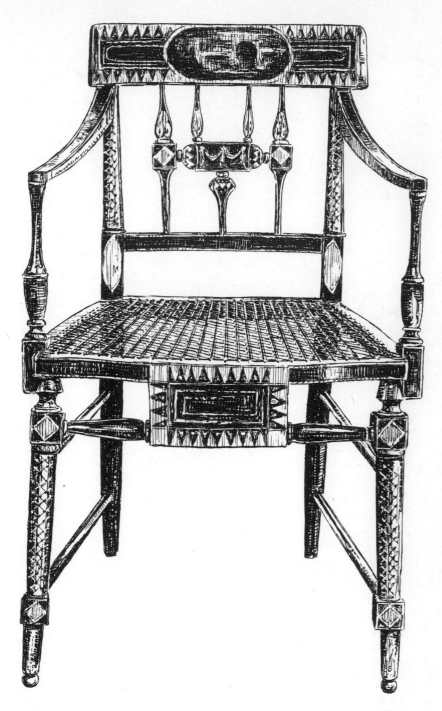

Fig. 138
PAINTED SHERATON chair from Baltimore
(The Henry Francis du Pont Winterthur
Museum, Winterthur, Delaware). The
ground color is deep red, the decoration
is mostly gold except for the scene
painted in various colors in the center of
the top rail.

CHAPTER SIX

Chairs of the Nineteenth Century

THE CLASSIC PERIOD (continued)

Grecian
Late Grecian (*Empire*)

TURNED CHAIRS

VICTORIAN

Fig. 139 GRECIAN CHAIR
presumed to have belonged to
DeWitt Clinton (1769-1828)
(Museum of the City of New York)

33. *GRECIAN* (*c.* 1805-*c.* 1840)

Mahogany

At Nehemiah Somes' Office No. 11, Kilby-Street [auction] A very extensive assortment of fashionable, elegant and common Furniture, consisting of . . . 1 Grecian Couch . . . 4 Grecian, 6 card, 5 Dining and 8 Pembroke Tables; 2 Grecian Stands . . . a great variety of Chairs, one set new, light and fashionable mahogany.

Columbian Centinel
(Boston) July 26, 1820

AFTER 1800 the trend toward classicism took on added momentum. Women styled their hair and their gowns like the women of ancient Greece and preferred their jewels in antique settings. They hung their curtains "in the Greek manner" and some of their dwellings had the columned porticoes of Grecian and Roman temples. America's infant villages were given such names as Sparta, Troy, Rome and Athens.

The population of the new American republic was growing apace, but in 1800 there were still only five cities with more than 10,000 inhabitants. New York, Philadelphia, Boston, Charleston and Baltimore were followed by Salem, Massachusetts, with 9500 citizens. New York, with 60,000, had nearly doubled its number in ten years and in 1803 DeWitt Clinton resigned from the United States Senate to become its mayor.

DeWitt Clinton was graduated from Columbia University in 1786, at the head of his class, and as New York's mayor he gave conspicuous service in organizing the public schools. He was still in office in 1812 when he was nominated for the Presidency and defeated by James Madison. In 1817 he became governor of the state.

Perhaps DeWitt Clinton is best remembered today as the driving force behind the project for the Erie Canal. When it was completed in 1825, New York celebrated with parades and pageantry. The first canal boat, carrying water from Lake Erie, was met by a fleet of ships and accompanied some distance into the Atlantic. There Governor Clinton symbolically poured the lake water into the sea. Three gold medals commemorating the event were sent to the surviving signers of the Declaration, John Adams, Thomas Jefferson and Charles Carroll of Carrollton.

An eagle is carved on the backs of chairs said to have been owned by DeWitt Clinton (Fig. 139). It was an ancient motif but had special meaning for citizens of the young nation. The eagle proudly decorated porcelain, glass and other household appurtenances, as well as articles of personal adornment. Clinton's eagle-back chairs are considered the work of Duncan Phyfe whose shop was on Fulton Street, west of Broadway.[1]

In 1784 the widowed Mrs. Fife had arrived from Scotland with her children, including sixteen-year-old Duncan.[2] They settled in Albany, but by the 1790's Duncan had gone to New York City where he changed the spelling of his name to Phyfe. After his superior cabinetmaking was noticed by the John Jacob Astor family, his furniture was in great demand. Phyfe's first work was in the Hepplewhite and Sheraton styles and his last in the Victorian, but his most outstanding pieces were in the Grecian style, a further development of the classic influence.

In France the Grecian style is called the Directoire and in England the Regency, though it does not exactly coincide with those political periods. Americans have given it a bewildering number of names (early Empire, early Federal, American Regency, American Directoire), but Grecian is descriptive and was one of the names used when it was made.

The *London Chair-Makers' and Carvers' Book of Prices* for 1802 listed Grecian legs (the sabre-curved front leg, Fig. 139), "Grecian Cross" chairs (Fig. 140) and Grecian couches, and also Roman and Egyptian chairs. Sheraton's *Dictionary* included chairs that he called Herculaneums, after the city buried by Vesuvius in 79 A. D. Few actual chairs were found in the excavations there or at Pompeii, but chairs were depicted on wall paintings, vases and sculptural reliefs (Fig. 145). In 1807 Britain's Thomas Hope wrote that France had "restored the pure taste of the antique Greek for chairs."

The chairs never exactly copied the ancient forms, but sometimes closely resembled them. Many of Duncan Phyfe's Grecian-style chairs are graceful,

Fig. 140
The "GRECIAN CROSS" is seen in the curved bars of the back and of the front legs (Harry Horton Benkard Memorial, Museum of the City of New York). Phyfe placed a gilded bronze mount at the intersection of the curved legs and also added gilded bronze feet.

sophisticated and trim. They have a sweep of curved line from the top rail to the floor, in front and in back (Fig. 141). The wide out-curving top rail is either veneered (Figs. 139-141) or carved in classic motifs.

Chair backs had diagonal cross bars, a carved slat (Fig. 142), a lyre splat (Fig. 141) and other patterns besides the eagle and "Grecian Cross." Seats usually were upholstered, occasionally caned. Phyfe made much use of reeding. He frequently carved his interpretation of the acanthus leaf on the front legs, but at times he carved the dog's leg, a motif the French had adapted from classic models.

[1] Charles Over Cornelius, *Furniture Masterpieces of Duncan Phyfe,* pp. 37-39.
[2] McClelland, *Duncan Phyfe and the English Regency,* p. 99.

Fig. 141
LYRE-BACK with a sweep of curved line
from the top rail to the floor (The Henry
Ford Museum, Dearborn, Michigan).
Phyfe's interpretation of the acanthus
leaf is carved on the legs, and also on
the legs of the DeWitt Clinton chair
(Fig. 139).

182

Fig. 142
GRECIAN chair made in New York, but not by Phyfe (The Metropolitan Museum of Art, New York City). It has spiral carving on the top rail and a carved slat in the back. This maker, like Phyfe, used reeding effectively.

183

Fig. 143 Late Grecian Chair
presumed to have belonged to
Alexander Telfair (1789-1832)
(Telfair Academy of Arts and Sciences,
Savannah, Georgia)

34. *LATE GRECIAN* (*c.* 1815-*c.* 1840)

(*EMPIRE*)

Mahogany, Rosewood,
Bird's-eye, Curly Maple

*Auctions . . . Blake & Cunningham . . . Furniture On Thursday . . .
at Concert Hall, Court-street,
A great variety of New Furniture consisting of 2 sets mahogany
Chairs with hair seats; 1 do. with cane bottoms; 1 elegant Sofa, covered with yellow Satin; 2 do. Chintz Covering; 6 sets fancy chairs.*

Columbian Centinel
(Boston) September 23, 1820

JAMES FENIMORE COOPER wrote, before 1828, that for some years "fashions and opinions from England" had been received "with great distrust" where
formerly "the influence of the mother country" had predominated "to an incredible extent." When Cooper dined at the White House with President Monroe he
found the drawing room "furnished in a mixed style, partly English and partly
French, a custom that prevails a good deal in the fashions of this country." It
was the War of 1812, rather than the Revolution, that turned Americans away
from England and toward France.

Thus it was that our countrymen were inclined to follow the French interpretation of neoclassicism, instead of the English, when it was in its full and
final swing before 1840. Their interest in contemporary Greece was heightened
when the Greeks fought for independence from Turkey between 1821 and 1827.

The architecture of this last phase of the classic period is called the Greek
Revival. Buildings patterned after the ancient temples were seen from Maine to
Georgia and in Ohio and other new western states. Domestic interiors strove for
grandeur and formality; rooms were spacious, ceilings high and statuary in
evidence.

One of the several Greek Revival houses in Savannah was built about 1818 by Alexander Telfair, for a home for himself, his mother and sisters. His father, the late Governor Edward Telfair, had made a fortune in East India trade, ship-building and other ventures. His sister, Miss Mary, who lived in the mansion until 1875, made provision for it to become the Telfair Academy of Arts and Sciences. Many of the original furnishings can be seen today by visitors to the Academy.

The furniture that the Telfair family ordered for their sixty-foot dining room was in the late Grecian style, the last style of the classic period and the one that frequently was influenced by French design. It has been called Empire, though it had scarcely begun when Napoleon's Empire crumbled following the Battle of Waterloo in 1815.

The furniture was scaled to the Greek Revival houses and was massive and austere. Heavy columns were seen on tables, sideboards and other pieces. Crotched-grain veneer covered plain surfaces. Mahogany was the leading wood, but bird's-eye and curly maple were used and rosewood was making its appearance.

Some of the decorative motifs in the coarse carving probably were inspired by Napoleon's Egyptian campaign and we find the sphinx, palm leaf and lion paw among them. At times the furniture was ornamented with gilded bronze appliqués, called mounts (Fig. 140), or, more often in this country, with gold stenciling that simulated the mounts.[1] The head and neck of the swan or goose were favorite figures for the arm supports of chairs.

Chairs were lighter in scale than other late Grecian furniture and better suited to small houses. As the factory system emerged they were made in great numbers. Their wide top rails sometimes extended beyond the stiles of the back (Fig. 146) like those on far older models (Fig. 145). The top rails were straight or shaped (Fig. 144) and in some instances were lightly carved. The chairs had low backs with either a wide splat (Fig. 144), often vase-shaped, or a slat, plain or carved (Fig. 143).

The refined curves of the early Grecian style were exaggerated in the late Grecian and lost much of their grace. This is noticeable on the Telfair chair. Most chairs had the sabre-curved leg of the early Grecian chair, but usually this leg had another curve near the seat that detracted from its trim line (Fig. 144). When legs were straight, they often were heavy and stodgy looking.

There were many cane seats, but more upholstered ones. The slip seat was covered with haircloth, cut velvet or other rich fabrics, not always new. An

Fig. 144
LATE GRECIAN or EMPIRE mahogany chair with low back, wide top rail and wide splat (City Art Museum of St. Louis). The legs are similar to the early Grecian, but have an additional curve near the seat.

author wrote of "the modern taste of turning the antique dresses of grandmamas into . . . drawing room chair covers."[2] If grandmother failed them they looked elsewhere. Lucy Hill's wedding furniture was being made by Nehemiah Adams of Salem, Massachusetts, in 1810, when she received a letter from a friend informing her, "I have purchased a brocade gown for your soffa at thirteen Dollars exactly Such a one as Rebecca Pierce gave fifteen for."[3]

[1] Janet Waring, *Early American Stencil Decorations,* p. 92.
[2] Elizabeth F. Ellet, *Women of the American Revolution,* II, 57.
[3] Hazel E. Cummin, *Handbook Concord Antiquarian Society,* p. 52.

Fig. 145
A chair depicted by the Greeks and Romans (from a photograph, courtesy of the Minneapolis Public Library). Other ancient chairs had legs similar to those in Figs. 140 and 143.

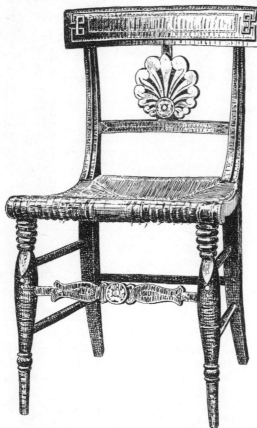

Fig. 146
LATE GRECIAN chair said to have belonged to *General William Clark* (1770-1838) of the Lewis and Clark Expedition (City Art Museum of St. Louis). It is painted green and gold, with a suggestion of a Greek fret on the top rail and a Greek anthemion in the back, and has a rush seat.

Fig. 147
FANCY chair from *Cleopatra's Barge*, a
yacht built in 1816 for **Captain George
Crowninshield** of Salem, Massachusetts
(Essex Institute, Salem). A marine scene
is painted on the top rail and small gilded
balls are seen between the slender cross-
rails of the back and in the front stretcher.

Fig. 148 BOSTON ROCKER
presumed to have belonged to
Ralph Waldo Emerson (1803-1882)
(Concord Antiquarian Society, Concord, Massachusetts)

35. *TURNED CHAIRS* (*c.* 1800-*c.* 1860)

BOSTON ROCKER, WINDSOR
SLAT-BACK, FANCY
Variety of woods

Wheaton and Davis, Fancy Chair Manufacturers, No. 153 Fulton-street, opposite St. Pauls Church, offer for sale, wholesale and retail, a large and elegant assortment of Curld Maple, plain painted and ornamented in gold & bronze, Bamboo, Plain and Gilt Balls, Rocking, Sewing, and Conversation Chairs . . .
Orders from any part of the continent executed with neatness and dispatch.
Old Chairs repaired, painted and ornamented.

New York Herald
October 29, 1817

SEVEN hundred of the minutemen who had "fired the shot heard round the world" on April 19, 1775, met in Concord two days later to hear a patriotic young preacher, the Reverend William Emerson. Soon he was to leave his manse* to become a chaplain and go off to Fort Ticonderoga never to return.

Sixty years afterward "eight or ten old gentlemen" who had fought on that April day were given seats of honor at Concord's two-hundredth anniversary. Ralph Waldo Emerson, grandson of William, was the orator for the occasion and proved himself a man "of distinguished talents and eloquence." He had been a clergyman like his father, grandfather and other generations before them, but he had resigned his pastorate in Boston before he was thirty. After traveling in Europe he had returned to Concord and to the manse of his grandfather.

In 1835 Emerson brought his bride to the large white house in Concord that he had just purchased. It was to be their home for the rest of their lives.* Gatherings there became an important part of the cultural awakening of New England. For a while Thoreau was a member of the Emerson household, the Alcotts were neighbors and Hawthorne lived in the old manse.

Emerson returned to Great Britain in 1847 and found that he had gained renown. He was much in demand for lectures and for social affairs. Among his friends in British literary life were Carlyle, Macaulay, Tennyson, Thackeray and Dickens. When the "Sage of Concord" was at home in Massachusetts, travelers from the world over came to see him just as they come today to see his house and his study.

Emerson's study has been moved to the nearby Concord Antiquarian Society, and those who visit it see the Boston rocker in which he liked to write with a portfolio on his lap. It is an early Boston rocker and has a scroll in the center of the top rail, rolled arms and a round, flat seat (Fig. 148).

Soon Boston rockers had seats that were rolled up in back and down in front. Later the scrolled top rail gave way to a more simple one with two semicircles cut from the lower edge. These changes facilitated mass production and before long the rocker, comfortable and inexpensive, was being sold in quantities throughout the nation. There is no evidence that it was first made in Boston, but it probably evolved from the high-back windsor rocker somewhere in New England shortly before 1825.[1]

The windsor chairs of the early nineteenth century are called Sheraton windsors because of their rectangular backs (Fig. 149). Bamboo turnings were customary. A later windsor much used in courthouses and other public places was a degenerate form of the early low-back. Ornamental turnings became extremely shallow or were missing entirely on late windsor and slat-back chairs. Sometimes even the finials disappeared from the latter.

The Shakers made the best slat-backs of the century. Their cabinetmakers were expected to produce only plain and useful furniture, but they worked with such skill and aesthetic appreciation that their chairs have charm as well as utility[2] (Fig. 150). At times they wove the seats of brightly colored tape instead of the usual splint or rush.

Fancy chairs were in high favor. Gilded balls between slender cross bars and a curved seat mark an early chair (Fig. 147). The Hitchcock fancy chair was first made by Lambert Hitchcock of Connecticut in 1826, but was copied in other factories. Seats were of rush, less often of cane and later of wood. Legs, frequently ring-turned, sometimes were splayed and the lower part of the front leg was bent outward (Fig. 151).

The fancy chair was decorated by an artist until about 1815, when stenciling began. The Boston rocker and the fancy chair were painted, most often black, then stenciled with bronze powders which came in several colors. The first fine stenciling was carefully shaded, but as the machine age gathered momentum the design became less delicate and the workmanship less meticulous.

[1] Walter A. Dyer and Esther S. Fraser, *The Rocking Chair*, p. 85.
[2] Edward D. Andrews and Faith Andrews, *Shaker Furniture*, pp. 103-9.

Fig. 149

SHERATON WINDSOR, so called because of the rectangular back (Shelburne Museum, Shelburne, Vermont). Some of these chairs had a single rather than a double top rail. The stretchers form an H as on earlier windsors.

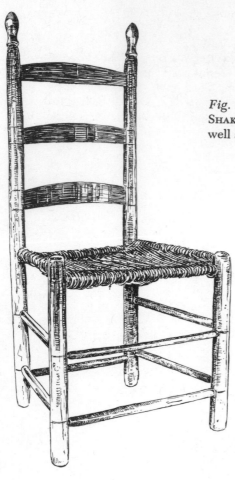

Fig. 150
SHAKER SLAT-BACK chair has charm as well as utility (Shelburne Museum).

Fig. 151
FANCY chair made by Hitchcock and given his name (Old Sturbridge Village, Sturbridge, Massachusetts). The back posts were shaved to give a better surface for stenciling; the legs are ring turned. The eagle, seen here and on the DeWitt Clinton chair (Fig. 139), was a popular motif in the new nation.

194

36. *VICTORIAN* (*c.* 1840-*c.* 1890)

Rosewood, Mahogany,

Walnut, Oak

H. T. Leeds, Auctioneer . . . No. 121 West Eighth Street on Tuesday, Jan. 16, at 10½ o'clock, the entire contents of said house, consisting in part of two costly superior rosewood suites, covered in satin brocatel, two elegant suits in silk plush; . . . carved rosewood centre and sofa tables, large pier and oval French plate mirrors, . . . carved rosewood and mahogany bedsteads, bureaus and washstands to match.

New York Herald
January 5, 1857

DURING the Civil War a small boy named Theodore Roosevelt became vaguely aware that his parents "were not one in their views" on the conflict, though they were devoted to each other. His father strongly supported Lincoln, and his mother, "a sweet, gracious, beautiful Southern woman," had brothers in the Confederate Navy. When the country was at peace again, the family left their New York City home for a year of travel in Europe. It was the first of Theodore's several sojourns there. He was a delicate child and was plagued with asthma, but he gained strength by persistent exercise and in his mature years had abounding energy and drive.

Contrary to the practice of most young men of means and social position at that time, Roosevelt went into politics. He was elected to the New York state legislature in 1881, a year after he had received a Phi Beta Kappa key and a degree from Harvard. Later, as his city's police commissioner, he made fearless and sweeping reforms in its most corrupt department. In the spring of 1898 he was Assistant Secretary of the Navy; that summer he was leading the Rough Riders in Cuba, and by fall he was governor-elect of New York. He became Vice-President, "an irksome, wearisome place," in 1901, and six months later he was in the White House.

Through the years Roosevelt loved nature and the out-of-doors. He was a rancher in the Bad Lands of North Dakota, a huntsman on four continents. Literature was another interest and somehow, despite his crowded days, he became the author of several volumes. His greatest joy was to be at his home, Sagamore Hill,* with his wife and six children, to whom he was a beloved companion.

The brownstone house that was Roosevelt's birthplace appears today much as it did when he was a boy and looked upon the parlor as "a room of much splendor." To him the prisms of its gas chandelier had "peculiar magnificence." Light-blue satin draperies, fringed and tasseled, hang over the lace curtains at the windows and the same satin upholsters the furniture. The carved marble fireplace, the tall gilt-framed mirrors and the accumulation of bric-a-brac are characteristic of Victorian interiors, yet this one has delicacy and restraint, whereas later rooms were cluttered, somber and overpowering.

The so-called Victorian style of furniture was in vogue most of Victoria's long reign, from 1837 to 1901. It took many forms, since this was a romantic age and furniture designers sought inspiration from a bewildering number of sources —medieval, oriental and Moorish, to name a few. No designer was as gifted in creating new patterns from diverse elements as Chippendale had been a century earlier. The chairs in the Roosevelt parlor (Fig. 152) are an adaptation of the style of Louis XV, the most admirable of all Victorian furniture (Fig. 154).

Overstuffed furniture was an innovation of the period and it was often tufted as was the upholstery on other pieces (Fig. 152). Before 1850 papier-mâché was in great demand. Chairs of this compressed paper were japanned before gay decorations were painted on them. Suites of furniture for the parlor or bedroom were still another innovation.

Such suites were made by John Henry Belter (1804-1863), an outstanding New York City cabinetmaker. One of the most fanciful of his rococo parlor sets has cornucopias, roses and other carved motifs (Fig. 153). Belter chose rosewood for the finest pieces and laminated thin layers of it (occasionally as many as sixteen) to give strength to his openwork carving.

This flamboyant furniture was in vogue on the Continent as well as in England and America and criticism of it was not long in coming. One of the most widely read denunciations was *Hints on Household Taste* by Charles Eastlake, first published in London in the 1860's. He deplored superfluous ornament and "the tendency . . . to run into curves. The faculty of distinguishing good from bad design," he wrote, "is a faculty most educated people—and women especially —conceive that they possess. How it is acquired few would be able to explain."

Fig. 152 VICTORIAN CHAIR
presumed to have belonged to
the parents of
Theodore Roosevelt (1858-1919)
(Theodore Roosevelt House, New York City)

Fig. 153
VICTORIAN chair from a parlor suite made by John Henry Belter of New York (Museum of the City of New York). Cornucopias and roses are among the carved motifs.

Despite his high-minded phrases, the Eastlake style of late Victorian furniture was often massive and grim-looking.

As the nineteenth century wore on, the machine became increasingly important, man's skill continually less. Factories turned out thousands of chairs in one pattern, machine made—even machine carved. No longer did a piece of furniture bespeak the artistry and the individuality of a certain master. Small wonder that surviving examples of the careful craftsmanship of long ago are given places of honor in our museums and in our homes.

Fig. 154
VICTORIAN OPEN-BACK chair, lightly
carved, with a modified cabriole leg
(Miss Adelaide Judkins, Hastings, Minnesota). This chair and the one in the
Roosevelt parlor (Fig. 152) are adaptations of Louis XV style.

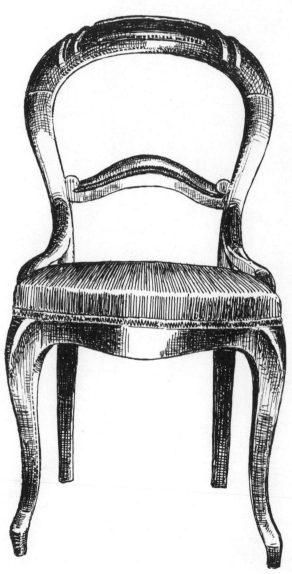

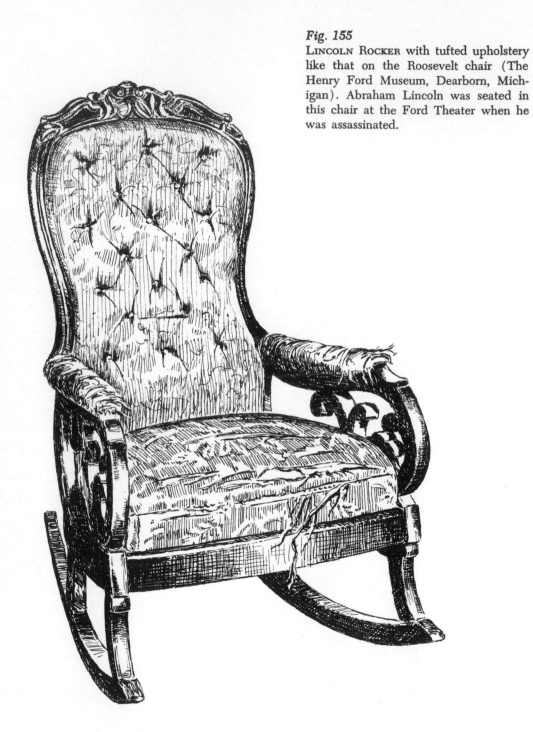

Fig. 155
LINCOLN ROCKER with tufted upholstery like that on the Roosevelt chair (The Henry Ford Museum, Dearborn, Michigan). Abraham Lincoln was seated in this chair at the Ford Theater when he was assassinated.

CHAPTER SEVEN

Chairs and Other Furniture Owned

by George Washington

Fig. 157
The earliest chair at Mount Vernon known to have belonged to
Washington. It is a Queen Anne-Chippendale transition chair
with a Queen Anne splat and trifid foot and a Chippendale top
rail and seat.

CHAIRS AND OTHER FURNITURE OWNED
BY GEORGE WASHINGTON

> *First in war, first in peace, and first*
> *in the hearts of his countrymen, he was*
> *second to none in the humble and endearing*
> *scenes of private life.*
>
> Henry Lee
> *December 26, 1799*

A MILLION and more visitors thread their way through Mount Vernon each year. Those who have some knowledge of furniture styles cannot fail to be struck with the fine eighteenth-century pieces that they see there. George Washington invariably asked for furniture that was "fashionable" or "in the newest taste," so he acquired in succession all the distinguished contemporary styles: Queen Anne, Chippendale, Hepplewhite and Sheraton.

There was some furniture at Mount Vernon when the twenty-two-year-old bachelor came into its possession in 1754, but he soon purchased more. Colonel Adam Stephen of Virginia made eight black walnut chairs for him in 1755,[1] but most of his furniture, before the Revolution, came from England. He shipped his tobacco there and in return received the greater part of his personal and household needs. Everything from a soup tureen to a marble mantel, from a letter seal to a chariot came across the Atlantic and to his door in vessels that left Britain bound for the Potomac.

Washington sent one of his first orders to England in April, 1757, from Fort Loudon where he was serving during the French and Indian War. Among other things he wanted "Two neat Mahogany Tables 4½ feet square when spread and to join occasionally" and "1 Doz'n neat and strong Mahogany chairs."[2] They

203

arrived in November on the ship *Peggy and Elizabeth*. The chairs were listed as the "best gothick chairs" (Chippendale) and had "Pincusion seats stufft in ye best manner and covered with horse hair."[3] He evidently had also placed a previous order, for in August of that same year the vessel *Salley* had brought him complete furnishings for a bedroom that had been purchased for him at an auction. Besides gilt sconces, a tea table, a "fine neat Mahogany serpentine dressing Table," and a bed with fluted posts, there were "6 Mahogany chairs, Gothick arched Backs . . . an Elbow Chair" and a "Mahogany easy Chair, on Casters."[4] The chair upholstery, bed hangings and curtains for three windows were all of yellow silk-and-worsted damask. The easy chair also had a slip cover of checked material.

In September, a month after this cargo had arrived, he sent to London for "one doz'n strong chairs" to replace some that were "neat but too weak for common sitting." The latter were to be moved to bedrooms and he wanted upholstery for them "of three different colours to suit the paper of three of the bed Chambers."[5]

Early in 1759 George Washington married Martha Dandridge Custis, a widow with two children whose estate, called the White House, was on the Pamunkey River in New Kent County, Virginia. For the next few months they continued to live there or at her residence in nearby Williamsburg, so that Washington could attend the House of Burgesses then in session. By April they were ready to leave for Mount Vernon and he sent word to a trusted servant to "get the Key from Colo. Fairfax's" and "to prepare in the best manner you can for our coming." Among other instructions the domestics were to "get out the Chairs and Tables, and have them very well rubd and Cleand."[6] Mount Vernon, then but a small house with four rooms on each of its two floors, was to put on a shining, spotless appearance for its new mistress. Within a few months Washington wrote that he was settled there "with an agreable Consort for Life" and that he hoped to "find more happiness in retirement" than he had "ever experienc'd amidst a wide and bustling World."

The young couple sent many lengthy orders to England, but there is no record that they bought additional chairs until 1764. That year "12 chairs covered with Leather and brass naild . . . 2 Elbows to ditto" and "6 Windsor Chairs painted Green" were received from London.[7] In 1765 "10 Mahogany chairs hair bottoms" and two matching armchairs were added to the accumulation at Mount Vernon.[8] George Washington apparently purchased more than seventy chairs in the decade between 1755 and 1765.

As far as is known, none of the furniture from these first English orders is at

Mount Vernon today. A Queen Anne-Chippendale chair there is one of the earliest pieces believed to have been owned by George Washington (Fig. 157).

The facility with which other types of furniture can be identified, as to style, when one is familiar with chairs is shown by a glance at Washington's slab or marble-top table (Fig. 158). It has the cabriole leg, somewhat elongated, and pad foot of Queen Anne chairs. By looking merely at the legs of an antique piece of furniture it is usually possible to tell the approximate time that it was made. This is not by any means the only way, but it is the easiest. If the legs of American chairs are kept in mind, as a rule anyone will be able to place an American table, bed or highboy, though pieces with the bracket foot, such as desks, chests of drawers and clocks do require further study.

Washington bought still more furniture in 1774, this time from the neighboring estate of Belvoir, owned by Colonel Fairfax who earlier had kept the key to Mount Vernon. The Colonel and his lady had sailed to England in 1773 to make their home there, and when their furnishings were sold Washington made several purchases. He listed them carefully: "4 Mahog^y. Chairs," a "Mahog^y. Card Table," "1 Mahog^y. Side board," and "12 Chairs & 3 Window Curtains from ye dining room."[9] A mahogany gaming table, possibly English and known to have been Washington's, is now at Mount Vernon (Fig. 159). It has the cabriole leg with the claw-and-ball foot and other marks of the Chippendale style. He also had a card table with the Chippendale straight leg and block foot (Fig. 160).

George and Martha Washington undoubtedly missed their friends at Belvoir. They had often dined together and had hunted the fox, attended balls and shared the other diversions of the countryside. But in any case the Washingtons' years of "happiness in retirement" at Mount Vernon were quickly to come to an end. England had closed the Boston port after the Tea Party which had stirred the colonists everywhere. Great changes were taking place on the political scene. On August 31, 1774, Washington noted in his diary, "Colo. Pendleton, Mr. Henry and I set out"—the representatives of Virginia were on their way to the First Continental Congress. Before they departed Mrs. Washington admonished Edmund Pendleton and Patrick Henry to "stand firm" and added, "I know George will." Less than a year later her husband was given command of the Continental Army.

General Washington seldom saw Mount Vernon during the Revolution. Mrs. Washington usually spent the winters at his headquarters and returned to Virginia when the campaigns opened in the spring. It is from an incident on one of her long journeys to and fro that we learn that crimson damask probably once upholstered chairs at Mount Vernon. When she traveled through New Jersey, she

Fig. 158
A marble-top Queen Anne side table with
a cabriole leg and pad foot like those on
Queen Anne chairs.

often stopped at the home of Colonel Charles Stewart. Once while she was there she proudly showed his daughter (a young widow whose husband had been on Washington's staff) two of her dresses made of cotton cloth woven at Mount Vernon. The colored stripes were made from ravelings of brown silk stockings and of old crimson damask chair covers.[10]

From Cambridge, the Heights of Harlem and many other headquarters the General sent detailed instructions to the man he had placed in charge of Mount Vernon. In spite of his efforts he later complained, "I made no money from my Estate during the nine years I was absent from it." He had added the library and the bedroom above it to his dwelling in 1774, and while he was away the addition of the banquet room had gone slowly forward. Soon after Washington returned home on Christmas Eve, 1783, a private citizen again, he began to make inquiries about finishing the interior of the banquet room. He was inclined to use "stucco" (plaster) below the chair rail, which he understood was "the present taste in

Fig. 159
A gaming table with oval depressions in the top for counters. The cabriole leg and claw-and-ball foot identifies it as Chippendale.

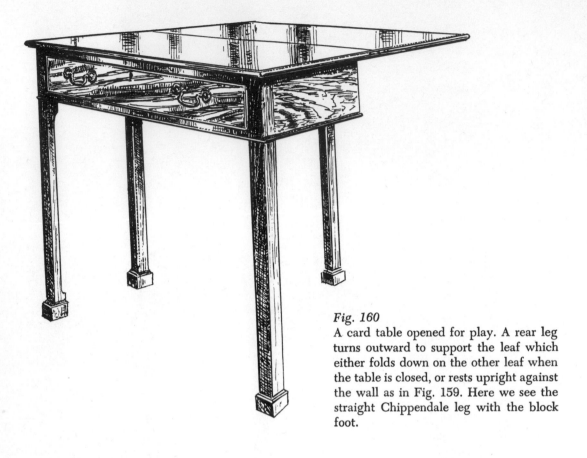

Fig. 160
A card table opened for play. A rear leg turns outward to support the leaf which either folds down on the other leaf when the table is closed, or rests upright against the wall as in Fig. 159. Here we see the straight Chippendale leg with the block foot.

England." Later he had it painted buff to match the woodwork. He wrote to Philadelphia to learn if plain blue or plain green wallpaper were available, as well as gilded papier-mâché borders to give these colors "a rich and handsome look."[11] In recent years bits of green wallpaper and wood-block paper border have been found beneath the later finishes given the banquet room. They have been reproduced and the room now has the original colors the owners chose for it. The twenty-four Sheraton chairs (Fig. 131), with their yellow haircloth seats figured in green, must have been both harmonious and elegant in the buff and green room.

Shortly before resigning his commission Washington had asked his nephew to find out, without mentioning his name, from "some of the best Cabinet makers, at which price, and in what time, two dozen strong, neat and plain, but fashionable, Table Chairs (I mean chairs for a dining room) could be had; with strong canvas bottoms to receive a loose covering of check, or worsted, as I may here-

208

after choose."[12] Five original Chippendale ladder-back chairs, now in the family dining room, are believed to be from this set (Fig. 161). These may be the chairs about which the General wrote in 1786. He had sent window curtains to Philadelphia to be dyed and he wanted "16 yards of Stuff of the same kind and colour of the curtains, to cover two dozen chairs."[13] Four ladder-back chairs of a different pattern, in this dining room, also are original. Other Chippendale chairs at Mount Vernon, owned by the Washingtons, include two pair with Gothic backs —one pair with the straight leg, the other with the cabriole (Fig. 162).

In the spring of 1784, a few months after his return home, Washington ordered "a dozn. and an half of Windsor Chairs" from Philadelphia.[14] Perhaps they were for the visitors who already were coming to him in numbers. This was twelve years before he purchased the "ovel" windsors for his piazza (p. 64). Three styles of American windsors that once belonged to him are to be seen at Mount Vernon today: the loop-back (Fig. 49), the fan-back and the hoop-back, including the Nelly Custis high chair (Fig. 163). The inventory of Washington's household goods, made after his death, lists one hundred and fifty-nine chairs; forty-five were windsors and thirty of them were on the piazza.[15]

General Washington had purchased a "fan Chair" in Philadelphia in August, 1787,[16] and a fan chair was in his library when his estate was inventoried. It was not listed as a windsor and possibly it was like the fan chair in Benjamin Franklin's study (p. 49) which Washington had had many opportunities to see and to use in that summer of 1787 when he attended the Constitutional Convention. He had called on Franklin as soon as he "got to Town" in May and he dined with him three days later. He made several other visits, once especially to see "a Machine at Doctr. Franklin's (called a Mangle) for pressing . . . clothes from the wash . . . well calculated for Table cloths and such articles as have not pleats and irregular foldings." The General was so taken with "the facility with which it dispatches business" that he later had one made for his own household. In 1788 he paid his friend Samuel Powel for an armchair that Mr. Powel had procured for him in Philadelphia. It was to be used "as a pattern."[17]

George Washington received official word, on April 14, 1789, that he had been unanimously chosen the first President of the United States. He soon set out from Mount Vernon on what proved to be a triumphal journey since he was welcomed ceremoniously all along the way. In New Jersey a majestic barge was waiting to convey him to New York where he was inaugurated on the last day of the month. A house had been taken for him at 3 Cherry Street, on a site now near the supports of the Brooklyn Bridge. When Mrs. Washington arrived on

May 28th she found the house "handsomely furnished all new for the General."[18]

But this dwelling proved to be both inadequate and inconvenient and the following February the Washingtons moved to the largest and most desirable mansion in the city. It was at 39 Broadway, about a block below Trinity Church, and had been vacated shortly before by the retiring French Minister, the Count de Moustier. Washington went there earlier to buy "some furniture of the Minister's (which was about to be sold, and was well adapted to particular rooms)."[19] His total expenditure was £665[20] and included the French furnishings of the green drawing room. In it were twelve armchairs, six "small" chairs and a sofa, all upholstered in green flowered silk. The curtains were of the same fabric.[21] One of the armchairs, in the style of Louis XVI, is seen at Mount Vernon today (Fig. 164). Another chair there, of the same style, came from the Château de Chavagnas, the birthplace of Lafayette.

The President also patronized New York upholsterers and cabinetmakers, particularly Thomas Burling who made him a writing desk, a bedstead, tables and three chairs. One of the latter was described as an uncommon chair and was priced at £7.[22] It is thought to be the "circular" chair (Fig. 167) which Washington valued at £7 in 1797.[23]

Soon after the President was comfortably established in the residence on Broadway, Congress voted to move the capital of the nation to Philadelphia. The Washington family, an aide-de-camp, a secretary and ten servants left New York at the end of August, 1790, making use of the vehicles and the sixteen horses that had been kept in the stables behind the house. They were bound for Mount Vernon where they planned to stay until their house in Philadelphia was ready for occupancy. Upon stopping there en route, they learned that the dwelling of Robert Morris, financier of the Revolution, had been selected for them. It was neither as suitable nor as "commodious" as the one that they had just left. The only place for the executive's office was on the third floor and Washington realized that all of his callers would "have to ascend two pair of Stairs, and to pass by public rooms, as well as private Chambers."

Tobias Lear, the President's private secretary, had remained in New York to supervise the moving of the household goods. He hired a carpenter who worked for seventeen days packing furniture, no doubt making use of the hay Mr. Lear bought for that purpose. Breakables were buried in bran, although one fragile ornament was packed in three pounds of cotton. When all was in readiness, the furnishings were put aboard the two sloops that had been rented to transport them to Philadelphia. The remaining servants also sailed on the two vessels, Washington's steward providing food for their passage. After Mr. Lear

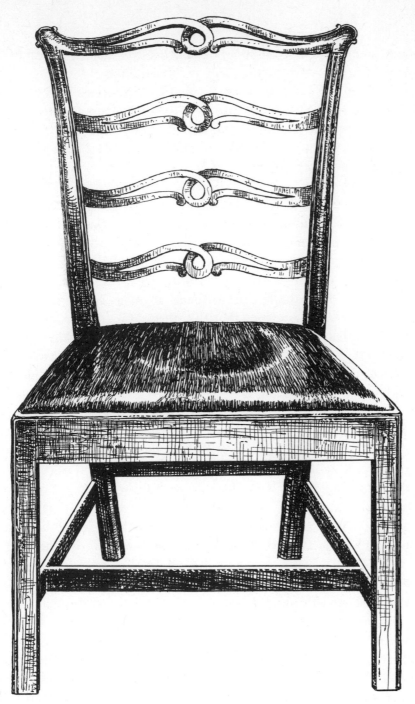

Fig. 161
This pretzel-back, straight-leg Chippendale chair is believed to be one of the "two dozen strong, neat and plain, but fashionable" chairs Washington ordered for the dining room. It has the slip seat "to receive a loose covering of check, or worsted."

had seen them off, he paid the outstanding bills and sold the two cows still in the stables. Then he and Mrs. Lear took the stage to Philadelphia.[24]

Fifty-eight cartloads of furniture were hauled from the two sloops to the Robert Morris house on High Street, now Market Street.[25] Washington frequently wrote Mr. Lear from Mount Vernon about the decoration of the house, the arrangement of the furniture and other diverse matters. As usual he was making careful, precise plans for his abode.

During the ensuing years he employed several Philadelphia craftsmen. In 1793, for instance, Thomas Smith was reimbursed for making two desks and for sundry "Jobs of Joiners work done for the year past,"[26] while Barteau, an upholsterer, was paid for six chairs and two stools to add to the furniture in the green drawing room.[27] Apparently "cha'r covers" were made in 1795 when thread and tape were bought for them.[28] "Blue & white furniture check"[29] purchased during the last week of the second administration seems to have been intended for Mount Vernon, but there is no evidence that this checked material was used for the covers of the "12 Chairs with Covers" in the west or blue parlor in 1802.[30] Household accounts through the years give testimony of Martha Washington's love for needlework. Chair cushions and other surviving examples of her skill are to be seen today at Mount Vernon.

When the President was about to retire, he made a list in his own hand of all of the furniture that belonged to the government. He recorded eighty-two chairs covered in yellow damask, an easy chair and seven sofas, three of which were upholstered in yellow. Most of the chairs were mahogany, ten of them were carved. Several dining room tables were listed as well as breakfast, tea, card and toilet tables. There were numerous beds, clothes presses and many other pieces.[31] When the capital was moved to Washington, D. C. in 1800, President John Adams took this furniture with him. It was destroyed when the White House was burned by the British in 1814.

Before leaving the Presidency in 1797, George Washington also itemized the furniture that belonged to him. He offered Mr. Adams his purchases from the Count de Moustier, at a reduction in cost. After thinking it over for some weeks, John Adams "declined, finally to take any part of the furniture in the Green drawing room."[32] It was put up for sale with other privately owned furniture that could not be used at Mount Vernon. A handsome Chippendale sofa, believed to have been purchased at this sale, is now in Independence Hall (Fig. 165). It has the paw foot and other marks of the richest work of Philadelphia craftsmen. Very likely it was made a number of years earlier, because by 1797 the Hepplewhite and Sheraton styles had been in vogue for some time.

Fig. 162
A Gothic-back Chippendale chair with
delicate carving on the top rail but none
on the knees of the cabriole legs.

Washington ordered a new desk from the shop of John Aitken of Philadelphia[33] and many who have visited Mount Vernon will recall this secretary in the library (Fig. 166). It is light in scale and has delicate inlay and other refinements of the Hepplewhite-Sheraton period. Washington bequeathed it and "the circular chair . . . an appendage of my study," (Fig. 167) to his "compatriot in arms and old & intimate friend Doct^r. Craik."[34] The secretary remained in the family of Dr. Craik, but one of his heirs gave the circular chair to Andrew Jackson. Both pieces were returned to Mount Vernon in 1905.

Two Hepplewhite chairs known to have been Washington's are at Mount Vernon; one has the five-feather and drapery design (Fig. 168). The bed in the first President's room was his own and is one of the three Mrs. Washington bequeathed to her grandson, George Washington Parke Custis, brother of Nelly. They were taken to Arlington,* the house he built across the Potomac from Washington, D.C. This bed has the square tapering leg and spade foot introduced by Hepplewhite (Fig. 169). Another bed at Mount Vernon, not a part of the original furniture, has the turned, reeded leg of the Sheraton style (Fig. 170). A Chippendale bed has either the cabriole leg or the straight leg, often with the block foot (Fig. 171).

Among the Hepplewhite-Sheraton tables owned by Washington are a dropleaf (Fig. 172) and a card table. Both are enriched with inlay. The sideboard also is inlaid (Fig. 173). From Mount Vernon it went to Arlington where it was used by Mr. Custis and later by his only child, who became Mrs. Robert E. Lee. Sideboards such as this were designed first by Thomas Shearer of England, a contemporary of Hepplewhite and Sheraton. They soon followed his lead. Earlier so-called sideboards, like one Washington bought at Belvoir in 1774, were merely tables placed at the side of a dining room. The first President acquired at least one set of Sheraton chairs (Fig. 174) besides the twenty-four made by John Aitken in 1797 (Fig. 131).

In 1878 Congress purchased Washington furniture from descendants of Nelly Custis Lewis and placed it in the Smithsonian Institution. It includes a pair of Hepplewhite armchairs once in the first executive's residence in Philadelphia (Fig. 175) and an easy chair left to Nelly by her grandmother (Fig. 176).[35] Mrs. Washington referred to it in her will as "the Great Chair standing in my Chamber."[36] According to family tradition it was the last chair in which George Washington sat.

At Mount Vernon there are many other admirable eighteenth-century pieces which supplement the original furniture so widely dispersed after the death of Martha Washington in 1801. The Mount Vernon Ladies Association, owner of

Fig. 163
The high chair used by Nelly Custis and her brother, George Washington Parke Custis, is a hoop-back windsor.

the estate since 1858, acquires well-documented Washington treasures as they become available. In this way the first executive's furniture, silver, china and other mementoes once more find their way to his home. The Association by its unceasing effort, including painstaking research, has brought Mount Vernon ever closer to the way it looked when George and Martha Washington presided over it.

After the inauguration of John Adams in March, 1797, the retiring President was thankful to be through, at last, with public life. He and Mrs. Washington and their entourage traveled slowly toward Mount Vernon. Perhaps they talked during the trip of their need of a new carpet for the blue parlor, because at Elkton, Maryland, after the second day's journey, Washington wrote Tobias Lear in Philadelphia asking him to buy one, preferably a Wilton. Two days later, in Baltimore, he wrote Mr. Lear about the carpet again. Since the furniture in the

215

Fig. 164
A French chair in the style of Louis XVI, believed to have been part of the green drawing room furniture of the executive mansion purchased from the Count de Moustier.

parlor was blue, "the ground or principal flowers in it ought to be blue also."[37]

Upon reaching Mount Vernon they found that it showed the "absence & neglect of eight years." The sloop *Salem* was to bring their belongings from Philadelphia, including some ninety-seven boxes, and Washington lost no time in finding workmen to prepare the "rooms for the furniture which is expected."[38] By April 3rd he was writing, "We are all in a litter and dirt, occasioned by joiners, masons, and painters, working in the house, all parts of which, as well as the outbuildings, I find upon examination, to be exceedingly out of repairs." He later wrote that the expense was almost as much as if he had "commenced an entire new establishment."

The illustrious couple, advancing in years, was content for the most part to remain under their own "vine and fig tree" and to enjoy the "rural amusements"

216

that they had missed for so long. Sometimes the first President attended affairs at Alexandria or visited the new District of Columbia and its "Federal City," not yet given his name. Once, when war with France was threatened, he was called to Philadelphia. But most always he tarried at Mount Vernon, managing its several farms, arranging his massive accumulation of papers and giving thoughtful attention to his dwelling. He entered into an agreement with Robert Morris and other gentlemen "not to quit the theater of this world before 1800," but he failed to keep it by a fortnight. George Washington had led an exemplary life in domestic concerns as well as in positions of public trust. His love for his home and his great pride in it will be a pattern for Americans—always.

[1] Worth Bailey, "Early Craftsmen," *Antiques*, February, 1945.
[2] *Writings of Washington*, ed. Fitzpatrick, II, 23.
[3] Eugene Prussing, *Estate of George Washington, Deceased*, p. 405.
[4] *Ibid.*, p. 405.
[5] *Writings*, II, 138.
[6] *Ibid.*, II, 318-319.
[7] Prussing, *Estate*, p. 408.
[8] *Ibid.*, p. 409.
[9] Gerald W. Johnson, Charles Cecil Wall, *Mount Vernon*, pp. 78-79.
[10] Elizabeth F. Ellet, *Women of the American Revolution*, II, 22.
[11] Johnson, Wall, *Mount Vernon*, p. 91.
[12] *Writings*, XXVII, 160.
[13] *Ibid.*, XXIX, 16.
[14] *Ibid.*, XXVII, 398.
[15] Prussing, *Estate*, pp. 410-448.
[16] *Writings*, XXIX, 258.
[17] *Ibid.*, XXX, 90-91.
[18] Stephen Decatur, Jr., *Private Affairs of George Washington*, p. 21.
[19] *Diaries of Washington*, ed. Fitzpatrick, IV, 84.
[20] Decatur, *Private Affairs*, p. 123.
[21] George Washington Manuscript, Library of Congress, Vol. 283, pp. 6-7.
[22] "Sundries—bo't on account of GW," photostatic copy, Mount Vernon.
[23] George Washington Manuscript, Vol. 283, pp. 6-7.
[24] Decatur, *Private Affairs*, pp. 153-158.
[25] *Ibid.*, p. 161.
[26] "Washington's Household Account Book, 1793-1797," *The Pennsylvania Magazine of History and Biography*, XXIX, 390.
[27] "Sundries—bo't on account of GW."
[28] "Washington's Household Account Book," *The Pennsylvania Magazine*, XXXI, 61.
[29] *Ibid.*, XXXI, 342.
[30] Inventory of Martha Washington's estate, Mount Vernon.
[31] George Washington Manuscript, Vol. 283, pp. 6-7.
[32] *Writings*, XXXV, 428.
[33] "Washington's Household Account Book," *The Pennsylvania Magazine*, XXXI, 347.
[34] Prussing, *Estate*, p. 58.
[35] Helen Comstock, "Mount Vernon Centennial," *Antiques*, July, 1953.
[36] Prussing, *Estate*, p. 390.
[37] *Writings*, XXXVII, 579.
[38] *Ibid.*, XXXV, 424.

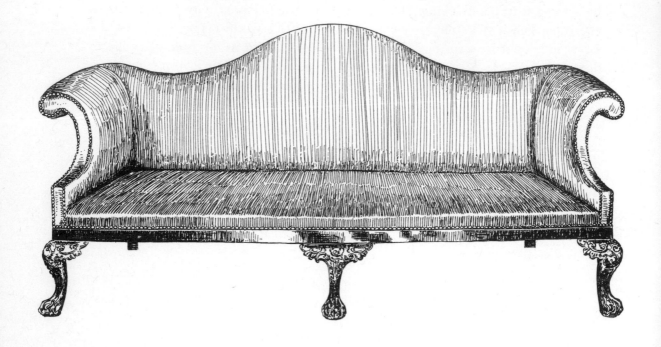

Fig. 165
A Chippendale sofa said to have been purchased at the sale of some of Washington's furniture upon his retirement from the Presidency (Independence National Historical Park, Philadelphia). The cabriole legs, with the rare paw foot, are intricately carved.

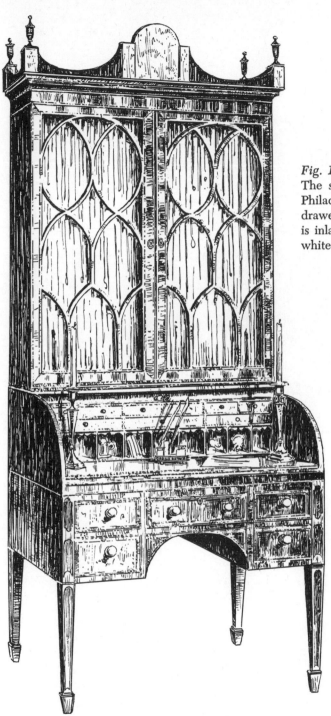

Fig. 166
The secretary made by John Aitken of Philadelphia. The two doors and all the drawers are banded with inlay and there is inlay on the square, tapering Hepplewhite legs with the spade foot.

Fig. 167
The circular swivel chair that Washington bequeathed, with the secretary, to Dr. Craik. Later it was given to Andrew Jackson.

Fig. 168
A Hepplewhite chair in a five-feather and
drapery pattern, with nail heads festooned
across the upholstery on the chair rail.

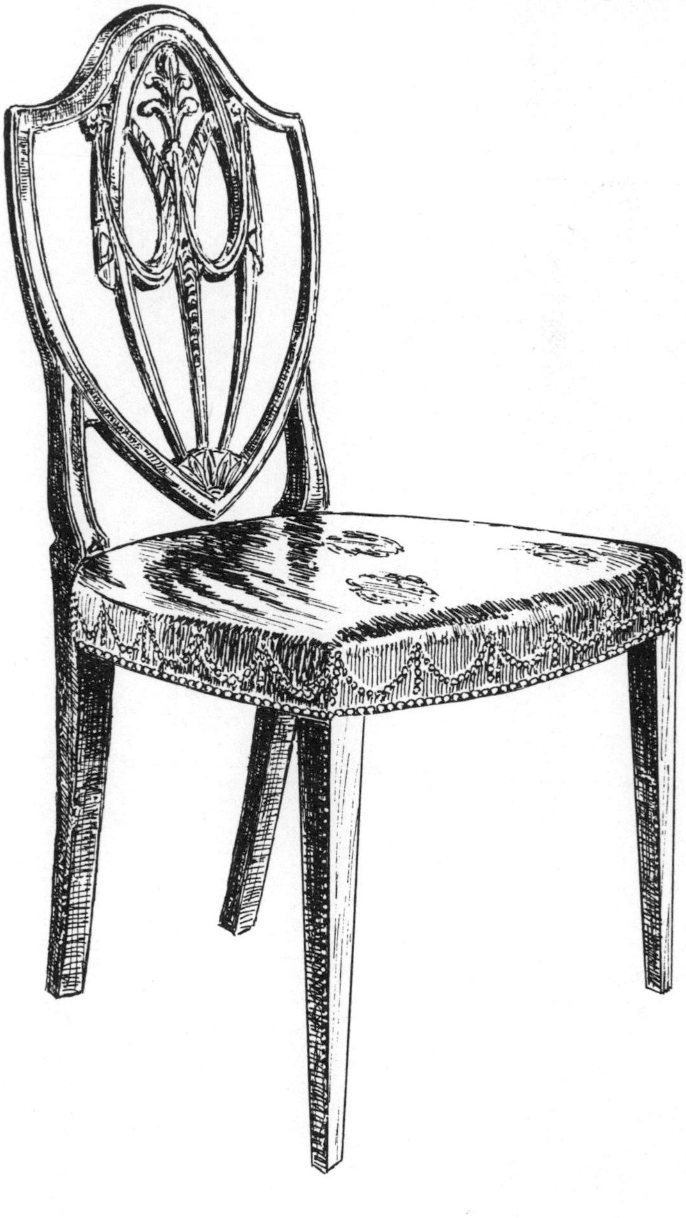

Fig. 169
A bed post from the bed in Washington's room has the square tapering leg and spade foot introduced by Hepplewhite. The brass medallion covers the bolt.

Fig. 170
A post from the bed in Nelly Custis' room has the reeded leg and turned foot of the Sheraton style. The upper post is reeded and carved. This is not an original Mount Vernon piece.

Fig. 171
Chippendale beds either had this straight leg, often with this block foot, or a short cabriole leg, usually with the claw-and-ball foot. (This bed with fluted and carved posts is not at Mount Vernon.)

Fig. 172
A drop-leaf or Pembroke table with satin-wood inlay on its slender, tapering Hepplewhite legs and more inlay on the frame beneath the drawer.

Fig. 173
Eight paterae are inlaid on this Hepplewhite sideboard. This piece, the Pembroke table and the Hepplewhite bed
were part of the Mount Vernon furniture that went to George Washington
Parke Custis. It was used at Arlington,
his estate near Washington, D.C., later
the home of his son-in-law and daughter,
General and Mrs. Robert E. Lee.

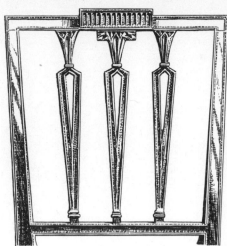

Fig. 174
Sheraton chairs of this design were purchased by Washington as well as the
twenty-four Sheraton chairs made by
Aitken (Fig. 131). This back has carving
on the top rail and on the three banisters.

Fig. 175
One of a pair of Hepplewhite armchairs
from the first President's residence in
Philadelphia. A rosette is carved at the
end of the arm (Smithsonian Institution).

Fig. 176
The Hepplewhite easy chair which Mrs. Washington bequeathed to Nelly Custis Lewis and described as "the Great Chair standing in my Chamber" (Smithsonian Institution). In 1878 Congress purchased this chair, along with other furniture including Fig. 175, from the heirs of Nelly Custis Lewis.

APPENDIX

(Museums and historic houses mentioned in the text that are open to the public, and places where many of the chairs in this volume are to be seen.)

CONNECTICUT
GUILFORD
Old Stone House (built 1639), Fig. 2
HARTFORD
Ætna Life Insurance Company, Figs. 59, 81, 88, 89
The Connecticut Historical Society, Figs. 35b, 39
Connecticut State Library, Fig. 113
Wadsworth Atheneum, Figs. 8, 17, 29, 76
MIDDLETOWN
Wesleyan University, Olin Memorial Library, Fig. 1
NEW HAVEN
Yale University Art Gallery, Figs. 109, 136; a Randolph sample chair, p. 124

DELAWARE
WINTERTHUR
The Henry Francis du Pont Winterthur Museum, Figs. 54, 55, 64, 80, 82, 95, 114, 138; p. 119; a Randolph sample chair, p. 124

GEORGIA
SAVANNAH
Telfair Academy of Arts and Sciences (built 1818), Fig. 143

ILLINOIS
CHICAGO
The Art Institute of Chicago, Fig. 120

MAINE
BRUNSWICK
Bowdoin College Museum of Fine Arts, Fig. 3
KITTERY POINT
Lady Pepperrell House (built *c.* 1760), p. 32

227

MARYLAND

MASSACHUSETTS

MICHIGAN

MINNESOTA

MISSOURI

KANSAS CITY
William Rockhill Nelson Gallery of Art, Atkins Museum of Fine Arts, Figs. 107, 116
ST. LOUIS
City Art Museum of St. Louis, Figs. 144, 146

NEW HAMPSHIRE

PORTSMOUTH
Moffatt-Ladd House (built 1763), Fig. 22; p. 64.

NEW JERSEY

ELIZABETH
Elias Boudinot House (built *c.* 1750), p. 107
MORRISTOWN
Washington's Headquarters (built 1774), Morristown National Historical Park, Fig. 23
PRINCETON
Princeton University, Firestone Memorial Library, Fig. 82

NEW YORK

EAST HAMPTON
Birthplace of John Howard Payne, author of "Home, Sweet Home" (built 1660), Fig. 38
JOHNSTOWN
Johnson Hall (built 1762), p. 97
NEW YORK CITY
The Metropolitan Museum of Art, Figs. 9, 56, 63, 65, 73, 104, 132, 142
Museum of the City of New York, Figs. 69, 139, 140, 153
The New-York Historical Society, Fig. 33
Theodore Roosevelt House, Fig. 152
OYSTER BAY
Sagamore Hill (built 1884), p. 196

NORTH CAROLINA

NEW BERN
Tryon Palace (built 1767), Fig. 75
WINSTON-SALEM
Old Salem, Fig. 48

PENNSYLVANIA

PHILADELPHIA
American Philosophical Society (built 1789), Figs. 45, 101, 102
Girard College, Fig. 126

Independence Hall (built 1745), Figs. 28, 43, 72, 91, 165
Philadelphia Museum of Art, Fig. 66; two Randolph sample chairs, p. 124
Powel House (built *c.* 1768), p. 85
Stenton (built 1730), pp. 81, 83, 119

RHODE ISLAND

PROVIDENCE
Rhode Island School of Design, Fig. 121

SOUTH CAROLINA

CHARLESTON
Heyward-Washington House (built 1750), Fig. 77
Middleton Place (gardens begun 1741), p. 117
Old Powder Magazine (built 1703), p. 117

VERMONT

SHELBURNE
Shelburne Museum, Figs. 149, 150

VIRGINIA

ALEXANDRIA
Woodlawn Plantation (built *c.* 1802), p. 165
CHARLOTTESVILLE
Monticello (built 1769-1809), Fig. 118
FAIRFAX COUNTY
Gunston Hall (built *c.* 1755), p. 119
FREDERICKSBURG
Kenmore (built 1752), Fig. 100
Mary Washington House, p. 133
MOUNT VERNON
Mount Vernon, Figs. 49, 83, 86, 105, 157-164, 166-174
WESTMORELAND COUNTY
Wakefield (built 1715, restored 1928), p. 133
WILLIAMSBURG
Bruton Parish Church (built 1710), p. 72
Colonial Williamsburg, Figs. 26, 57, 58, 103; a Randolph sample chair, p. 124

WASHINGTON, D. C.

Smithsonian Institution, Figs. 4, 6, 30, 78, 122, 131, 175, 176

BIBLIOGRAPHY

Andrews, Edward D. and Faith, *Shaker Furniture*. New Haven, Yale University Press, 1937.

Aronson, Joseph, *The Encyclopedia of Furniture*. New York, Crown, 1938.

Bissell, Charles S., *Antique Furniture in Suffield, Connecticut, 1670-1835*. Connecticut Historical Society, Suffield Historical Society, 1956.

Bjerkoe, Ethel Hall, *The Cabinetmakers of America*. Garden City, New York, Doubleday, 1957.

Bond, Harold Lewis, *An Encyclopedia of Antiques*. Boston, Hale, Cushman and Flint, 1937.

Bridenbaugh, Carl, *The Colonial Craftsman*. New York, New York University Press, 1950.

Burroughs, Paul H., *Southern Antiques*. Richmond, Garrett and Massie, 1931.

Burton, E. Milby, *Charleston Furniture, 1700-1825*. Charleston, South Carolina, Charleston Museum, 1955.

Carpenter, Ralph E., Jr., *The Arts and Crafts of Newport, Rhode Island, 1640-1820*. Newport, Preservation Society of Newport County, 1954.

Chamberlain, Samuel and Narcissa, *Southern Interiors of Charleston, South Carolina*. New York, Hastings House, 1956.

Cornelius, Charles O., *Early American Furniture*. New York, London, The Century Company, 1926.

Cornelius, Charles O., *Furniture Masterpieces of Duncan Phyfe*. Garden City, New York; published for the Metropolitan Museum of Art, Doubleday, Page & Company, 1922.

Dow, Charles Francis, *Every Day Life in the Massachusetts Bay Colony*. Boston, Society for the Preservation of New England Antiquities, 1935.

Downs, Joseph, *American Furniture, Queen Anne and Chippendale Periods in the Henry Francis du Pont Winterthur Museum*. New York, Macmillan, 1952.

Dyer, Walter A., *Handbook of Furniture Styles*. New York, London, D. Appleton-Century Company, 1936

Dyer, Walter A., and Fraser, Esther Stevens, *The Rocking Chair—An American Institution*. New York, London, The Century Company, 1928.

Halsey, R. T. H., and Cornelius, Charles O., *A Handbook of the American Wing*. New York, The Metropolitan Museum of Art, 1924.

Hipkiss, Edwin J. *Eighteenth-century American Arts, The M. and M. Karolik Collection*. Cambridge; published for the Boston Museum of Fine Arts, Harvard University Press, 1941.

Hornor, William Macpherson, Jr., *Blue Book, Philadelphia Furniture, William Penn to George Washington.* Philadelphia, 1935.

Kettel, Russell Hawes, *The Pine Furniture of Early New England.* Garden City, New York, Doubleday, Doran & Company, 1929.

Lichten, Frances, *Decorative Art of Victoria's Era.* New York, Scribners, 1950.

Lockwood, Luke Vincent, *Colonial Furniture in America.* 2 vols. New York, Scribners, 1913.

Lyon, Irving W., *The Colonial Furniture of New England.* Boston, Houghton, Mifflin & Company, 1891.

McClelland, Nancy, *Duncan Phyfe and the English Regency, 1795-1830.* New York, W. R. Scott, Inc., 1939.

Miller, Edgar G., Jr., *American Antique Furniture: A Book for Amateurs.* 2 vols. Baltimore, 1937.

Morse, Frances Clary, *Furniture of the Olden Time.* The Macmillan Company, 1902.

Nagel, Charles, *American Furniture, 1650-1850.* New York, Chanticleer Press, 1949.

Nutting, Wallace, *Furniture of the Pilgrim Century.* Framingham, Massachusetts, Old America Company, 1924.

Nutting, Wallace, *Furniture Treasury,* 3 vols. Framingham, Massachusetts, 1928, 1933.

Nutting, Wallace, *A Windsor Handbook.* Saugus, Massachusetts, 1917.

Ormsbee, Thomas Hamilton, *Early American Furniture Makers.* New York, Thomas Y. Crowell Company, 1930.

Ormsbee, Thomas Hamilton, *Field Guide to Early American Furniture.* Boston, Little, Brown, 1951.

Ormsbee, Thomas Hamilton, *The Story of American Furniture.* New York, The Macmillan Company, 1934.

Sack, Albert, *Fine Points of Furniture: Early American.* New York, Crown, 1950.

Winchester, Alice, *How to Know American Antiques.* New York, Dodd, Mead & Company, 1951.

INDEX

Bold-face numbers indicate pages on which biographies and definitions of specific terms will be found.

Comb-back, 60; fan-back, 60; hoop-back (bow-sack), 55-56; loop-back (balloon-oval), 64; low-back, 55, 56; New England, 64; Sheraton, 192
    Legs, 56, 60; feet, 60
    Seat, 57, 60; upholstered, 64
    Spindles, 60, 64
    Stretchers, 60
    Turnings, 60, 64, 192
    Upholstery, 64
    Wood, 57, 64; painted, 64
Chairmakers, 72, 87, 99, 109, 155; *see also* Craftsmen
Chair-table, 11
Chaise longue; *see* Couch
Châlons, France, 39
Chambers, Ephraim, 139
Chamfer, **57**
Charles I, 71
Charles II, 4, 27, 28, 71
Charles II chairs; *see* Chair styles, cane
Charleston (S. C.), 64, 71, 104, 114, 117, 119, 134, 179
Charlestown (Mass.), 52, 71
Charlottesville (Va.), 149
Charter Oak, Hartford (Conn.), 4
Chase, Samuel, 143
Château de Chavagnas (Lafayette birthplace), 210
Cherry (wood), 64, 76; *see also* Section headings
Chestnut (wood), 109
Chests (furniture), 4, 9, 205
Chew, Mary; *see* Paca, Mrs. William
Children's chairs, 42
China, 83
China; *see* Porcelain
Chinese influence, 64, 83, 114, 119
Chippendale style, 87, 160, 196, 204, 205, 209, 212; *see also* Chair styles
Chippendale, Thomas, **94**, **95**, 99, 104, 119, 124, 134, 140, 196; *see also* Books of furniture designs
Chippendale, Mrs. Thomas, 94
Chippendale, Thomas II, 95
Church of England, 21
Cicero, works, 144
"Circular chair," 210, 214
Cities: population in 1800, 179; style changes in, 29, 140
Civil War, 195
Clark, General William, Fig. 146
Clarke, Nathaniel, 39
Clarke, William, 22
Classic influence, 140, 150, 156, 160, 166, 179, 180, 181, 185, 186
Classic period, 137-189
Clinton, DeWitt, **179**, **180**
Claw-and-ball foot, 83, 109, 205; *see also* Foot
Clocks, 205
Clothes presses, 212
Coach, 87
Coastal cities, 29, 171
Colonial Williamsburg, 71, 72, 76
Colors (of chairs, chair upholstery, dress, house interiors), 22, 28, 32, 43, 45, 52, 64, 83, 104, 127, 128, 134, 155, 156, 172, 174, 196, 204, 205, 206, 212
Columbia University, 128, 179
Commode, 83, 104

Commonwealth, English, 22
Concord (Mass.), 191, 192
Concord Antiquarian Society, 192
Concord, Battle of, 140, 192
Confederate Navy, 195
Connecticut, 3, 4, 140, 192
Constitutional Convention, The, 49, 114, 127, 153, 209
Continent (European), 3, 27, 28, 196
Continental Congress, The, 53, 93, 103, 107, 109, 113, 114, 117, 123, 127, 139, 143, 153
Contrivances for chairs, 49, 50, 128, 209
Cooper, James Fenimore, 185
Corner chairs, 104, 105
Corwin, George, 17, 45
Couch, 28, 32, 41, 42, 45, 83, 172, 180
Craftsmanship, 87, 99, 124, 192, 198, 208
Craftsmen (cabinetmakers, carvers, chairmakers, joiners), 4, 27, 29, 65, 72, 87, 94, 95, 99, 100, 109, 123, 134, 140, 144, 146, 150, 155, 172, 180, 192, 196, 198, 203, 208, 210, 212, 214
Craik, Dr. James, 214
Crests, **32**, 42, 45; *see also* Top rails
Crewelwork; *see* Needlework
Cromwell, Oliver, 22
Cromwellian style; *see* Chair styles
Cross bar, 160, 181, 186, 192; *see also* Cross rail.
Cross rail, 45, 72; *see also* Rail
Crowninshield, Captain George, Fig. 147
Cupboard cloths, 39
Cupboards, 4, 10, 39
Curtains: bed, 39, 43, 45, 128, 134, 204; window, 39, 45, 128, 134, 179, 196, 204, 205, 209, 210
Cushion stools, 4; *see also* Stools
Cushions, 41, 45, 155, 212
Custis, Eleanor or Nelly (Lewis, Mrs. Lawrence), 165, 166, 209, 214
Custis, George Washington Parke, 165, 214
Custis, John Parke, 165
Custis, Mary Ann Randolph; *see* Lee, Mrs. Robert E.
Customs, 29, 76, 140, 171, 185
Cutler, Reverend Manasseh, 49
Cyma Curve, 87

Daily Post, London, 76
Dating furniture, 29
Davis, Benjamin, 72, chairmaker
Davis, Charles K., Fig. 115
Day bed; *see* Couch
Declaration of Independence, 59, 60, 93, 113, 117, 123, 139, 144, 180
Delaware, 27, 93, 124, 155
Delaware River, 27, 93, 123
Dennis, Thomas, 4, joiner
Derby, Elias Hasket, 144, **171**, **172**
Derby, Elizabeth; *see* West, Elizabeth Derby
Desk chairs, 105
Desks, 123, 205, 210, 214
Dickens, Charles, 191
Dictionary, Indian, 21
Digges, Mrs. Elizabeth, 43
Directoire, American (style), 180
Directoire, French (style), 180
Disbrowe, Nicholas, 4, joiner
Documents, 9, 29, 59, 99, 107; *see also* Labels of cabinetmakers
Dog's leg, 181

Sheraton, 160; Queen Anne, 72, 76, 87; windsor, 60, 64; *see also* Rail, semicircular
Topsfield (Mass.), 11
Trade, 29, 31, 76, 93, 103, 104, 139, 159, 171, 172, 186, 203
Transition chairs, 72, 94, 140, 150, 205
Triangular chair; *see* Chairs, triangular
Trifid foot, 83, 94
Trinity Church, New York City, 210
Trinity College, Dublin, 3
Trumble, Francis, 56, chairmaker
Tryon, Governor, Fig. 75
Tufft, Thomas, Fig. 76, cabinetmaker
Turkey, 185
"Turkey Carpets," 41
Turkeywork; *see* Needlework
Turkish carpets, 22
Turned foot, 45, 51, 104, 166
Turner, 11
Turnery, 10, 11
Turnings, 17, 42, 45, 51, 52, 60, 192
Turnings, types of: ball, 17, 45; ball-and-block, 22; ball-and-ring, 22, 60; bamboo, 64, 192; inverted cup, 72; mushroom, 17, 45; ring, 192; sausage, 52; trumpet, 72
Turrell, Rev. Ebenezer, 10
Tyler, John, 71
Tyng, William, 23, 45

United States of America: Congress, 210, 214; flag, 171; furniture owned by, 212; Senate, 143, 179
Upholders, 134; *see also* Upholsterers
Upholstered chairs: Chippendale, 128, 134; Cromwellian, 22; Hepplewhite, 172; leather, 32, 72; Queen Anne, 83; Sheraton, 172; Victorian, 192; George Washington's, 204, 210, 212, 214
Upholsterers, 134, 210, 212
Upholstery: leather, 22, 64, 72, 83, 128, 150, 155, 204; sealskin, 22; tufted, 196; *see also* Textiles

Valley Forge (Pa.), 143
Van Rensselaer family, 99
Vase-shaped splat, 72, 76
Vendue (auction), 75, 139, 204
Veneer, 76, 87, 181, 186
Venetian blinds, 134
Vernon, Admiral, 133
Vessels; *see* Ships
Vesuvius, Mount, 180
Victoria, Queen, 196
Victorian style; *see* Chair styles
Virginia, 29, 31, 43, 63, 71, 75, 76, 119, 133, 146, 149, 153, 203, 204
Virginia, University of, 149
Virginia walnut, exported, 76
Voltaire, 85

Wainscot, 4; chests, 4, 19; cupboards, 4; walls, 4, 127; *see also* Chair styles
Wakefield (birthplace of George Washington), 133
Wallpaper, 119, 127, 134, 156, 204, 208

Walnut, 27, 32, 34, 64, 76, 87, 104, 203; *see also* Section headings
Walpole, Horace, 9
War of 1812, 159, 185
Warren, General Joseph, Fig. 68
Warren, Nathaniel, 11
Washington, Augustine, 133
Washington, Mrs. Augustine (Ball, Mary), 133, 134
Washington, Betty; *see* Lewis, Mrs. Fielding
Washington, John, 133
Washington, George, 53, 63, 64, 71, 87, 103, 107, 113, 123, 133, 139, 143, 150, 153, 155, 165, 203-6, 208-10, 212, 214, 217
Washington, Mrs. George, 63, 64, 113, 123, 166, 172, 204-6, 209, 210, 212, 214-16
Washington, Lawrence, 133
Washington, Martha Dandridge Custis; *see* Washington, Mrs. George
Washington, Martha, Chairs, 172; *see also* Chair styles, Sheraton
Washington, Mary Ball; *see* Washington, Mrs. Augustine
Washington, D. C., 155, 212, 217
Waterloo, Battle of, 186
Web foot, 83
West, Benjamin, 85, 117
West, Elizabeth Derby, Fig. 127
West Indies, 31, 104, 159
Weyman, Rebecca, 134, upholsterer
White House, 153, 185, 195, 212
White House (home of Martha Dandridge Custis), 204
Wicker chairs, 17, 18
William III, 71
William and Mary style; *see* Chair styles
William and Mary College, 59, 71, 75
Williams, Roger, 21, 22
Williamsburg (Va.), 59, 71, 72, 75, 76
Willing, Elizabeth; *see* Powel, Mrs. Samuel III
Wilmington (Del.), 124
Windsor chairs; *see* Chair styles
Windsor, England, 56
Windsor, English chair, 56
Wingohocking, Chief, 81
Wing chair; *see* Chairs, easy
Winslow, Mary, 22
Winston-Salem (N. C.), Fig. 48
Winterthur Museum; *see* Henry Francis du Pont Winterthur Museum
Winthrop, John Sr., 3, 21
Winthrop, John Jr., 3, 4, 43
Winthrop, Mrs. John Jr., 43
Woodlawn (home of Lawrence and Nelly Custis Lewis), 165, 166, 174
Woods used; *see* names of wood; *see also* Section headings
Wren, Sir Christopher, 71
Writing chairs, 60, 64, 105
Wright, Will, 11
Wythe, George, 59

Yale University, 107
Yoke-shaped top rail, 72, 76